CHURCH MUSIC IN THE NINETEENTH CENTURY

CHURCH MUSIC IN THE NINETEENTH CENTURY

by

ARTHUR HUTCHINGS

GREENWOOD PRESS, PUBLISHERS
WESTPORT, CONNECTICUT

Library of Congress Cataloging in Publication Data

Hutchings, Arthur, 1906-
    Church music in the nineteenth century.

    Reprint of the 1967 ed. published by H. Jenkins,
London, in series: Studies in church music.
    Includes bibliographical references.
    1. Church music--England--History and criticism.
2. Church music--Protestant churches. 3. Music
--History and criticism--19th century. I. Title.
II. Series.
[ML3131.H88 1977]   783'.026'09034   77-7920
ISBN 0-8371-9695-7

Originally published in 1967 by Herbert Jenkins, London

Reprinted with the permission of Barrie & Jenkins

Reprinted in 1977 by Greenwood Press
a division of Congressional Information Service
88 Post Road West, Westport, Connecticut 06881

Library of Congress Catalog Card Number 77-7920

ISBN 0-8371-9695-7
Printed in the United States of America

10 9 8 7 6 5 4 3 2

Contents

Preface

I LACK courage to forgo this traditional opportunity to forestall criticism, for I have discovered that if the subject upon which I so readily agreed to write were comprehensively surveyed, even in a small book, I should need more time and travel than I can afford for several years to come. It was easy to mention what was sung in Vienna at Schubert's church in 1815, and surely it would not be difficult to find out what was sung that year at the Sistine Chapel, Notre Dame and Westminster Abbey; but what was sung forty miles away at Kuckucksdorf am Donau, Paese di Cuculo, Coudrette les Coucous and Little Cucking? An exercise bombastically called research, but accurately called prying into cupboards and pestering friends, leaves my answers still vague; I *think* I know the sort of music that served the south German and English village.

I accepted quickly when Dr. Routley suggested that I should write about a subject which included the music by which I first tasted heaven, when neither gramophone nor radio could take me to concert or opera. In those days country folk and most townsfolk heard the music they made among themselves, and little more. If much of it now seems trivial or sentimental let us be glad that it served its day so well, for those who used it progressed towards better music. After all, what brought new thousands to play and sing it? The answer cannot be denied by those who tell us that most of it was bad and that it was badly performed, for the answer is simple—new zeal where, early in the century, worship had been careless and comatose.

7

Very little church music after Bach's is superfine, for it has rarely been the medium of a superfine composer's ambition unless his temperament and appointment, like Bach's, has made it so. The bulk of church music scarcely survives its composers. I was prepared to write about the music still used and admired except by fashion-following coxcombs, but if I examined thoroughly what has not survived I should keep the publisher waiting for a very stodgy tome. It seems more sensible to supplement knowledge with imagination and to declare any indulgence in guessing. The decision incurs much "I suppose" and "As far as I know" but this unscholarliness is better than impersonal sciolism.

Here, then, is no professional *Beitrage*, but some account of nineteenth century church music undertaken by the assistant organist at St. Oswald's, Durham, the parish once served by one of the most devoted incumbents to have earned a niche in the musical pantheon—Dr. J. B. Dykes. I wanted to dedicate these pages to Canon Kenneth Meux with whom I shared the task of providing simple music at St. Oswald's, for I never worked with a vicar whose restraints and encouragements proved wiser, nor with one who more effectively secured the combination of seemliness and homeliness in the conduct of services. Yet he would agree that the dedicatees should be Mgr. Paul Grant, President of Ushaw College, and the Vice-President and Choirmaster, Mr. Laurence Hollis. My protestant tongue does not falter at "Father Hollis" but Ushaw proudly recalls the style of address brought from Douai and still used in this country during the penal years. These gentlemen saved me time and expense by showing me manuscript music used by the college from about 1780 to 1830 and a wealth of printed music used since. Good company and music, some by no means sacred, give me rare holidays on evenings when I have time to go up to Ushaw, and I am deeply grateful for Monsignor's invitation to invade without knock or notice. His unfussing kindness shall not make me forget the honour of this privilege.

CHURCH MUSIC IN THE
NINETEENTH CENTURY

I

Optimism and Gusto

We hear more sermons on faith than on hope, without which faith lacks radiance. Most outstanding men of the nineteenth century were such optimists that they either forgot the Devil or treated him as a medieval superstition. Two vast wars have since then set carpenters and clerks killing and maiming carpenters and clerks, few of whom wished to kill and maim; they could acknowledge their contribution to human error but could they reasonably believe that the horrors they witnessed were the just retribution for their sins? The wars "came"; evil overtakes us because evil is with us. Are we who know that so mean that we cannot admire those whom we envy even in their delusions? We need not share the liberal vision, the optimism that inspired men from Mirabeau and Beethoven to Whitman and Wagner, whose music belies this professed pessimism, but we shall surely not peevishly deride the panache of music and poetry during most of that splendid century.

The romantic agony of which we are so fond of talking was no bleak despair but a luxurious yearning for the unattainable—at the least a passion, as in *Tristan*, at the greatest a religious aspiration as in Bruckner's symphonies and masses. When emotions are ardent their alliance with a religious mind makes for intense devotion. After the eruption of the French Revolution and Napoleon our forebears believed ardently in human betterment, not just human prosperity; the century was one of religious revival and philanthropy; its expression could be fine or vulgar but it is capital which we still spend. No music of ours has yet moved vast numbers of us unless it owed something to theirs.

Forced to mention the main achievement of western civilisation during the past century many would choose the advance of nations towards political democracy, and with it the rise of such institutions as trades unions and co-operative trading. Though none of the larger churches moved notably towards lay counsels in its government, yet social changes were reflected in their worship. At the opening of the century services were dominated by the person and voice of the officiant at the altar, desk or pulpit; by 1860 this was not usual in most churches. Congregations had already been vocal in Lutheran and Methodist communities but chiefly in hymnody which was usually led by a choir—not the kind appointed to perform liturgies vicariously but the kind now familiar almost everywhere as leading congregational praise. "The Parish Choir" was the name of a monthly magazine which flourished during the middle years of the century; its pages were concerned less with hymnody than with liturgical matter (not just in Sunday services but weddings, funerals and red-letter weekdays) that had once been either the concern of the officiant or had been said, except in cathedrals and collegiate churches.

The spread of congregational hymnody and responsory, together with the formation of choirs to lead it, caused the most obvious change in protestant church music during the century; and since hymnody made increased infiltration into Roman Catholic devotions there was a greater difference in public worship between 1800 and 1900 than between the extremes of any previous century that had passed without a major religious upheaval. Yet it is our duty first to discuss music that is rarely used in services, music which claims highest classification because it came from great composers whose technical advances are ultimately at the service of the many minor talents which supply most of the music for church, home, school and entertainment. The time taken for talent to

catch up with genius must be added to the time lag of conservatism, for even in a matter like formal dress conservatism is
a mark of respect and would affect a public ceremony even if
it were less important than public worship. This time lag is
not to be deplored; it militates usefully against fashion, the
requisition of new styles, strongly associated with this or that
place or activity, for church and worship in a way that might
be stunt.

Why, apart from reasons given earlier, should the very great
composers from Beethoven to Bruckner have made so small a
contribution to church music? The question initiates controversy since the ready answer, that nineteenth century styles
were more unsuited for worship than most, is a shallow
generalisation. It is true that many trends of thought and
expression since 1789 have not helped artists to identify their
most exalted conceptions with the restraints of contemplative
devotion or traditional ritual. The vividly dramatic works of
Berlioz, Beethoven, Liszt and Verdi, which a general historian
would call the century's finest tributes to Christian ideas, are
among the least congruous with official ideals of church
music: Berlioz's *Requiem* and *Te Deum* are almost inconceivable
in church and they were originally performed in public
squares. Yet parts of the same composer's beautiful triptych
L'enfance du Christ have been heard in churches although the
complete work is a series of humanitarian tableaux such as
might please atheist as well as Christian; if, however, such
music were allied to a liturgical text it would surely be better
church music than most because it came from an outstanding
imagination. The few pieces by supremely great composers
which happen to be used in small churches—Handel's hymn
tune "Gopsal", some of Bach's contributions to Schemelli's
Book, Byrd's "Lullaby my sweet little baby" or his "Ave
verum corpus", Victoria's "Jesu dulcis memoria", the less
difficult church works of Purcell or Schütz—do not these stand
out as special treasures in quite a different class from the many
serviceable pieces composed just to meet demand? Of course

the great composer's works do meet demand or we should not use them, but they meet it indirectly, not at the bidding of recommendations. Genius meets its own demand first, albeit inspired by text and context, so that its sacred offering has the same personal stamp as its secular work. Genius does not change musical style, don the mantle of piety and change its personality to keep sabbath.

Sincere writers have erred by declaring that composers should use for church a different *style* than for school, theatre, concert or home. (I do not now contradict my comment on Berlioz's *Requiem* and *Te Deum*.) The error is increased by assessing the styles of different historical periods according to their appeal to our own worship in *general*, placing the nineteenth century lowermost in esteem and the eighteenth next, despite the fact that churches use much music from these two centuries and find that it wears well. Style is judged by a total form to which melody, harmony, texture, rhythm, treatment of a medium, etc., are contributory, and if the formulae of one of these contributors mar a total integration of style we risk the effect that distresses us when "unto" and "vouchsafe" are interlarded with idiomatic modern usage. Deliberately to cultivate a church style is to fill churches with repository "art" instead of work that differs from Beethoven's or Fauré's only in scale and difficulty. The nineteenth century has too often been arraigned for the secularity of its church music instead of for its popularising of much inferior composition; it has rarely been arraigned for initiating a fault that arose, as so often, from one of its notable achievements. It began the revival of much medieval, renaissance and baroque music, especially that of Palestrina and of Bach; bound up with scholarship and admiration of what the scholars revealed came the producing of what may be called cultural music, to be admired for its evidence of the composer's education in older music rather than his urgent expression. Now the hidden springs of musical invention may find a catalyst in admiration of old music—they did in Bach himself as in his admirers, Mendelssohn and Brahms—but no excellent music was yet composed by trying to do what Byrd or Bach did better or by expecting scholarship and culture to compensate for an inferior imagination and invention. Our professors of music are not our great composers. If they were so they should be blamed for spending the time in teaching, writing, organising and committee-sleeping that they could give to laying the all-too-few golden eggs.

My declaration does not accord with the sentimental opinion that fine secular expression can always be consecrated for church. If we do not know whether an unfinished building is a skating rink, school, swimming bath, crematorium, abattoir, factory, library or church, the architect lacks faith, imagination or both. Church music should of course be appropriate to whatever occasion or ritual it purports to serve—solemn at a consecration, gay as a carol or stirring as a march in other contexts. We are more sensible in judging secular than sacred art. We are melted by Handel's Cleopatra, Berlioz's Dido and Wagner's Isolde; but we do not set up Berlioz's chaste and noble expression of love as "more appropriate" to a generalisation called "opera" than the warmer, more libidinous music of Handel or Wagner. Is it not rather conceited to suppose that a Victorian knelt before a poorer conception of God than mine, or that he envisaged a less worthy church service? The woolly harangues and ugly prayers of our time, the many disappointing buildings and musical compositions which we must try out before we secure recognisable fine things—these need not depress us, but they tell us that we no more possess artistic reward for sincere intentions than did our predecessors.

Our mistakes and successes show us the right approach to theirs. We fail most when we adopt a consciously modish expression as a substitute for imagination, when we manufacture the acceptably churchy. Our successes, from fine tunes to Epstein's *Majestas* or Messiaen's organ pieces, do not snap the fingers at traditional aids to devotion or the feelings of simple churchfolk, but neither are they born of respect for official directives as to the proper styles for church art, as if one ought to *adopt* styles. Fine church music is simply fine music which happens to be evoked by a fine artist's love (maybe temporary love) of some theme common to himself and churchmen, and from congruity with place, purpose and performing conditions. These qualities become increasingly apparent the better we know the work. The bad music of the nineteenth century is less often inappropriately secular than falsely sacred, for its composers set out to elicit from their hearers or singers what they supposed to be a devotional attitude—a dangerous favourite phrase used by writers of church music and by the hierarchy in directives.

The vehicles of *religioso* change with other stylistic changes. The nineteenth century opened in the high summer of the classical symphonists and the dawn of the new romantic opera so that religious decorum could be observed by recourse to the staider rhythms and contrapuntal textures of the baroque. Theoretical tribute was paid to the modes but deference to them was almost unrecognisable by the ear. (Bach's "Dorian Toccata and Fugue" are in D minor and our copies may even give us a B flat in the signature.) In this early part of the century we rarely find what are now thought to be sanctimonious turns of harmony or phrase even among German Pietists. The diminished sevenths and chromatics with which Bach met the sighs and "Ah!"s even on festal days in Neumeister's "new model" cantata texts would have been used for a tortured Prometheus or an abandoned Dido; they were not exclusively religious. Plenty of eighteenth century music is sentimental but nowhere does it give us quite the unction of "O rest in the Lord"—a weak item in a splendidly dramatic oratorio. Bach does not suggest complacence to us when expressing comfort (in the limited sense, not the theological) during the last chorus of the *St. Matthew Passion*, where the feminine cadences and other turns of harmony remind us of Mendelssohn—not surprisingly, since Mendelssohn thought this chorus a model.

Mendelssohn was a manly and witty creature in whom had been instilled so great an obligation of public service in return for wealth and ability that he most certainly hastened his death by overwork. It is well to remember the amount of music by him which is not sentimental, as well as the amount that is being rediscovered (e.g. some of the string quartets) and found passionate. He was certainly not the parent of the nineteenth century brand of "churchiness" in music; that unctious harmonium style can be traced back to Vienna—conventionally religious Vienna of the Congress pageant, fast making money to pay for the wars and Napoleon and fast bleeding its visitors. Beneath the pretty surface which for musicians is reflected in Lanner's waltzes or even the lighter piano pieces and songs of Schubert, Vienna was more vicious than any capital city—not from any special wickedness of her citizens but because she was now in decline from the most musical of capitals to the one offering most light music as the premier pleasure-city. There was a similar decline from the Venice of the Gabrielis and Monteverdi, seventeenth century Venice, to the Venice of Vivaldi and Galuppi which soon became only the summer resort of German and English voluptuaries, at best a glorified Brighton or Blackpool; the decline of Vienna was more swift.

Now it is precisely among the non-religious that false-religious styles are loved. What organist has not been asked to play sentimental pseudo-religious ballads at the weddings of people who are not seen normally at worship? The unctuous style we hear every Christmas in song and dance "hits" about "Mary's little baby" (more revolting than the most wilfully lewd ditty) is found in church music by Schubert and the Chevalier Neukomm, both known in private letters to be agnostic. To find its apogee one had best avoid controversy about *Parsifal* but to point to certain works by Richard Strauss, so brilliant a professional that he could turn on many styles, including the expression of Christian ideas which he abjured. What he associated with them is all too patent from his *hôtel splendide* vision of blissful futurity in *Tod und Verklärung*. The secular music in *Salome* is no longer revolting and was probably never as shocking as its first hearers pretended. (Our St. Oswald's

Mothers' Union and Girl Guides can put on a floor show to a record of the "Seven Veils" that makes the last few Covent Garden Salomes and their attendants seem as vestal virgins.) The really disgusting music is the uplift, as our American friends would call it, of Jokanaan's chantings from the cistern— as disgusting as a senatorial candidate inevitably dragging "Gard" into his election speeches. Fortunately most productions afford enough amusement from the cistern, the severed head, and Salome's callipygous transports to overlay disgust at the religiosity. It is not in the deeply religious Dykes that one finds revolting sanctimosity but in the charmingly worldly Sullivan. If Sullivan had simply applied the fresh melody and skilled technique of "Brightly dawns our wedding day" to a carol, or concentrated what he squandered upon *The Golden Legend* into one good setting or anthem, if above all he had shown himself in church music to be the master of the extended complex, needed for the finale of an operatic act—in short, if he had not felt the need to be a different Sullivan on Sundays, he might have contributed something enduring to church music.

Yet we must be very careful in music as in life before saying "Hypocrite". More than once in history good men have disparaged their predecessors' approach to the sanctuary. As a boy I heard baroque and rococo churches called "theatrical" if they were Roman Catholic and "four-square preaching boxes with gaudy plaster" if they were Protestant. Today we are taught to admire fanes built in the last decades of feudalism when the church was still regarded as God's Palace if not *teatrum sacrum*, to note how its altar or pulpit is dramatically placed and the music of its time such as should be offered to *The* Grand Seigneur; we are reminded, not only by Addleshaw who coined the phrase, of the good sense of Wren's "auditory church" and it is a long time since I heard any depreciation of even late eighteenth century churches. Are we ready to examine nineteenth century art by the ideals of those who made it for their own use? Should posterity bother the church composer or artist? He should surely work for the kind of worship he knows and loves. My grandmother, having sampled this or that town church, rustled home in tussore and ospreys and declared with great content "The music was *most* elaborate and the sermon *most* eloquent!" Is it entirely to our credit that her testimony today would be thought sarcastic? As we review music of the nineteenth century let not our queasy minds despise its gusto and panache.

2

Contributions by the Great Composers

If this were a catalogue this chapter would fill about a quarter of a page—not because most great composers were non-Christian, for in fact most of them reckoned themselves churchmen. Nor should the churches be blamed for the few contributions they secured from great composers; rather should most denominations be praised for shifting away from the aridity of the age of reason and the tacit belief that their primary duty was to justify the ways of God to man in sermons and writings. As the nineteenth century moved past its middle years there grew almost universally the contrary beliefs either that fervent worship was more important than instruction or that effective instruction should lead to devout worship. Oh that such beliefs were more widely held in this century when even newly proposed orders of service are full of oblique harangues, from haranguing of the baby to be baptised to haranguing of the corpse to be buried or burnt! Not even the Roman Church maintains its good example, for we have "Instructional masses" during which we wonder whether we should listen to what is being said at the altar, what is being sung by the choir or what is being endlessly explained and farced by the instructor in the pulpit or aisle.

The small contribution of great composers to church music during what is known in histories of music as The Romantic Period (roughly from 1830 to 1890) can be attributed to what will be called hereinafter the reconciliation problem—reconciliation between the romantic imagination and the traditional demands of a public liturgy, however liberally interpreted. Churches awaking from torpor were not quite prepared for the dramatic vividness of the new composers. Reconciliation did not worry Beethoven, Schubert, Weber or Dvořák, but it plainly worried others.

BEETHOVEN

Beethoven's only church music, consisting of two masses, is "most elaborate", disregarding the standard Viennese lengths and treatments of items which had been established by the Reutters, father and son, each an esteemed imperial kapellmeister. By comparison with the *Missa solemnis in D*, the earlier C major seems a small work, but it is lengthy and very fine. We still hear it on special occasions such as the Christmas Eve midnight mass.[1] The great Mass in D seems to be on a scale unthinkable for liturgical use, yet it was composed expressly for the consecration in 1821 of Beethoven's friend and patron, the Archduke Rudolph, as Archbishop of Olmütz in Cologne Cathedral. It underlines at every strikingly original passage some point of doctrine which the composer had carefully pondered, for he would set nothing which he could not believe. The unexpectedly heavy treatment of "et" as clauses follow in the Credo implies "And this, too, I accept". The single alteration of the ritual is an insertion of "Ah", later altered to "O", before an occurrence of *miserere nobis* in the Gloria. What seemed at the time of composition to be the most unearthly melody and harmony, that of the lydian mode, Beethoven reserved for *Et incarnatus est* (Ex. 1) to honour the mystery which the mass is declared to prolong. This unique setting of the mass strained even Beethoven's ability and it therefore contains defects; it will suffice to mention only one— fugue subjects recalcitrant both to the texture they initiate and

[1] In Austria, Rhineland, Hungary, Poland, south Germany and beyond their frontiers local permission to use the orchestra seems never to have been withheld despite the 1903 discouragement of wind and percussion instruments.

the instruments they are destined to engage. During many of this man's finest works we are aware that he and the performers are at grips with materials that cannot be perfectly mastered to convey neatly what they convey so powerfully, yet by their imperfection we reach to the sublime as we cannot during an accomplished artefact of smaller aim. We misunderstand both

Ex. 1

Ex. 2

Ex. 3

Beethoven and catholic teaching if we describe the *Mass in D* as "merely humanitarian" because of such phenomena as an *Agnus Dei*, which is labelled "A prayer for inward and outward peace", and the menacing suggestion of distant war which is brought into the music to symbolise this conception. Humanism and Christianity are not exclusive, and to substitute "humanist" for "atheist" or "rationalist" is tendentiously erroneous or cowardly.

SCHUBERT

The only two of Schubert's masses to become popular in churches were his second and third, in B flat and G respectively, composed in 1815. They are short and bright, somewhat resembling Haydn's shorter masses, and such passages as the empty, lilting *Dona nobis pacem* at the end of the B flat work recall Haydn's apology which I quote in Geiringer's version: "I become so cheerful at the thought of God that he surely will not blame me for praising Him with a cheerful heart"; but we recall it inappropriately, for there is no evidence that Schubert was religious. He had a good friend in the music director of the Liechtenthal Church and probably received more commendation from his neighbours for his orchestral masses performed there than he did for his greater orchestral and chamber works. Most parts of Schubert's masses from the G major onwards are excellent Schubert. I should mention their popularity in England later in the century. They were edited by Berthold Tours as "Schubert's Communion Services" but printed with the Latin as well as an English text. Since this was long after the death of Novello's original proprietor their publication pays tribute to their appreciation outside the Roman Church. Tours was assisted by the choirmaster of St. Mary's, Clapham, Thomas Gale, who "revised Schubert's underlay of the sacred texts without interfering with the harmony", quoting a decree approved by Leo X which forbade "every piece in which words are omitted, deprived of meaning or indiscreetly repeated" and "every piece which detaches versicles that should be connected". Why mention this edition of 1894 when Schubert died in 1828? Because none of Schubert's works was widely known until Schumann discovered the scores and bought them from the composer's brother, a poor schoolmaster who was glad to be paid for them.[1]

Quotations from Schubert's greater masses (Ex. 2) show

---

[1] No Schubert symphony was performed in England till 1856. Mendelssohn merely rehearsed one.

early traces of a malady that was to affect great and small church musicians—mechanical recourse to chromatics which had been exquisitely sweet in Mozart's hands but less so in his Viennese disciple, Spohr. Schubert rarely indulges in adventitious pathos except in the so-called *Deutsche Messe* in F of 1826, composed for an evening service that was popular in southern Germany during Advent and Lent. The German text used by Schubert had also been used by Michael Haydn at Salzburg. Prayers and instructions were interspersed with items of the mass to vernacular words, usually associated with oratorio and opera, a fact which tended to elicit an indulgence in subjective human emotions.

Tender expression is too often condemned where it is justified by context and does not sound stale. Judgment in this matter will need such constant exercising as we meet the music to which our age is in natural reaction that we ought to discuss it at once while we are dealing with the great composers. At Ex. 3 will be seen the opening of one of Schubert's songs; it is slightly pathetic with a vernal tenderness, for the song is called "Dreams in Springtime". There is no exact parallel to this music before Schubert, yet the melody and harmony is so simple that one wonders why it could not have occurred in a piece by any of Schubert's predecessors, despite the fact that its inspiration may have been his unconscious recollection of a similar melody at the opening of Beethoven's "Spring Sonata" for violin. Lacking precise terms we call this vein of sentiment romantic. The sweetness is of honey, not of saccharine. Let us turn to a minor composer who has been too glibly called sentimental. The most pathetic hymn tune of J. B. Dykes also contains no chromatics, and its vocal parts are worthy of Gibbons. I refer to *St. Cross* found at *E. H.* 111 and *A. and M.* 113.[1]

---

[1] This tune is wasted upon Faber's "O come and mourn", which contradicts scriptural and therefore catholic teaching. "Weep not for me, daughters of Jerusalem, but weep for yourselves." The solemnity of Good Friday does not incur pity for a Saviour who, we are told, came to the world specifically to perform the acts of Good Friday as the first stage in the victory celebrated on Easter Day.

The word "romantic" leads to slippery ground, for the most imaginative of the early romantics, Berlioz, has been called sexlessly chaste in his expression. Propose any quality as romantic—subjective emotion, freedom from formality, enterprise in design—and ask in what age it is not found in great composers. We may think Handel's tenderness to be healthy and hearty, but its first hearers may have thought it more heart-felt than hearty, or even febrile at times. Why go only

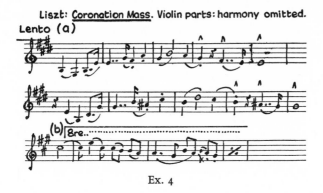

Ex. 4

to Handel? Why not to Monteverdi of Tubal Cain? The secrets of our hearts are exposed by Sophocles and Shakespeare; they reveal our psychoses as do Hugo and Wagner. "All art is romantic in its own day" wrote Stendhal, and thereby deprived the epithet of distinction. It becomes a nuisance unless we agree that it shall refer only to the evocative music[1] of the nineteenth century.

It is true that much romantic music expressed private emotions which are often out of place in the contexts of worship, and the reconciliation problem I have mentioned became tougher as the subjective emotions acquired a large part of symphonic and choral expression. Their most notable alliance with religious ideas and large-scale design was Wagner's *Parsifal*

[1] I lack patience to discuss here the connotations of "romantic". I have tried to do so briefly in Vol. 3 of *The Pelican History of Music*.

which had an almost wholly bad effect on church music and minor composers generally. Even a sincerely devout man like César Franck, being strongly influenced by Wagner, failed to leave behind any enduring settings of the liturgy. On the other hand we have slender grounds for objecting to the sentiments in church music by Berlioz, Schubert, Weber and early romantic composers unless we also question those in church music by Haydn, Mozart and Beethoven. Schubert has been called "the last of the giants" and is normally classed with the other three great "Viennese" classics rather than the German romantics; Einstein in his *Music in the Romantic Era* calls him "the romantic classic".

WEBER

Carl Maria von Weber, 1786–1826, is often named as the first of the German romantics, chiefly on account of his student songs, *Lyre und Schwert*, and his operas *Der Freischütz* and *Euryanthe*; in the latter magic effects, haunted woods, legendary knights and medieval ladies replaced the classical personages and scenes of eighteenth century operas; they appealed to Schubert who was doomed never to find the right librettist or to succeed in the theatre as did the musician "born on the stage". Weber's romantic success leads us to forget that he died before Schubert, indeed before Beethoven; yet his church music belongs to the classic era and thus postpones the romantic problem. An author who sounds queerly anglican tells us that Weber's masses are "unfortunately not in the pure style". For some time I was puzzled by this word "pure" in hierarchical pronouncements and in those of Cecilian Societies which arose during the middle years of the nineteenth century, disliked flamboyant church music and favoured the restoration of sixteenth century polyphony as well as the adoption by composers of styles for worship that caused minimum association with opera and the secular concert. I then remembered that a particularly stupid schoolmaster had once puzzled me with the same word; when I reached years of lust I assumed that by "pure" he meant "chaste". I therefore assume that the Cecilians also meant "chaste" but were also vulgarly genteel. Whatever they meant their vocabulary shows muddled thinking. There is no great music in a pure style because all great music is indebted to previous music; I do know a little great music which might be thought chaste but it is certainly not by Palestrina, most of whose music sounds sumptuous unless it is badly sung and interpreted; it probably sounded even more sumptuous in the churches which first used it. The queer feature of our author's strictures on Weber's masses, however, is that he should suppose them "impure" yet use no adverse epithet towards the church music of Haydn, Mozart and Beethoven.[1]

As the Dresden kapellmeister[2] Weber composed the more grandiose of his two masses, that in E flat, to honour the jubilee year of the Saxon King's reign. There is a larger measure of Weber's operatic lyricism in his G major mass of 1819 which is also worth occasional hearing. Weber's masses do not quite equal Schubert's but they show a quality lacking in workaday composers who have little experience of writing long secular pieces. Beethoven surely had this quality in mind when he shrewdly said "Weber should write operas—many operas", for Weber commanded deft transition from and to disparate musical ideas. This ability is required in the efficient setting of a story with contrasting characters and rapidly changing situations; it served Weber excellently in a long asymmetrical text like *Credo*.

[1] René Aigrain: *La musique religieuse*, Paris, 1950. This epicene vocabulary seems to be growing. I recently heard a bishop talk about "having sex", of all fatuous expressions! Neither the catholic fathers nor the protestant reformers who gave us our English liturgy would have feared the plain word "rut", but our modern effeminate liturgiologists have even changed the splendid "I will neither follow them nor be led by them" (meaning the Devil's guiles) for an incredibly soppy and inexact substitute.

[2] The office of kapellmeister had become virtually that of opera conductor and composer. Weber's successor, Wagner, wrote no church music, for which we may be grateful. The chorales in *Die Meistersinger* are effectively allied with English hymns at *E. H.* 313 and *Songs of Syon* 149.

BERLIOZ

The great composers we have so far discussed, being within the classical tradition of liturgical music, were scarcely aware of its restraint upon the romantic imagination. Schubert's magnificently contrapuntal motet *Intende voci orationis meae* (later much admired by the Cecilians) seems to come as easily from him as his lyrical offertories or his unaccompanied but by no means pastiche-like Palm Sunday antiphons. Berlioz was unaware of any reconciliation problem, too, for we cannot regard as church music his sacred pieces for state occasions. His *Grande Messe des Morts* was for the victims of the July Revolution of 1830 and his *Te Deum*, begun 1849, for a national tribute to Napoleon. These works could have been composed only by a Frenchman of catholic upbringing but his own words ban them from church—"The text of the Requiem was for me a long-coveted prey at last delivered into my hands"—"My *Te Deum* is Babylonian, Ninevite . . ." This *Te Deum* needed a thousand participants, including six hundred children and brass bands which outblast those of the Requiem, in which work the wilful mingling of words from the Proper with words from the Ordinary removes at a stroke any thought of liturgical propriety. We therefore do not encounter the reconciliation problem in great composers until we reach two of utterly differing temperament, Mendelssohn and Liszt.

MENDELSSOHN

Mendelssohn, 1809–1847, actually wrote settings of the anglican canticles among which the *Te Deum* in A is particularly grand, but they are too long for the cathedral daily repertory and are for mixed voices with soloists. They were intended chiefly for local choral festivals. Naturally his best church music shows its Lutheran provenance and includes pieces based on chorales, a set of eight-part unaccompanied anthems (so entitled) for different seasons, three works called motets of which only *Veni Domine* is well known in this country as "Hear my prayer", and cantata-like psalms, of which the most impressive are Psalms 42, 95, 98, 114 and 115. Mendelssohn's church music was composed between 1830 and 1846; Liszt's, which is so extensive as to require six pages of Grove for its mere catalogue, was composed between about 1855 and 1885; though it includes commissioned works based on Lutheran chorales, e.g. *Nun danket* for the dedication of an organ at Riga, these are vastly outnumbered by masses, canticles, introits, sequences, settings of *Tantum ergo, Salve Regina* and *O salutaris Hostia* and other requirements of Roman Catholic services. Compared with Mendelssohn's church works they show how the reconciliation problem hardly troubled a Roman Catholic until late in the century yet affected a Protestant before 1850. Today we should expect the reverse.

Dannreuther's statement that Mendelssohn's Psalms were "for the concert room" and his motets and cantatas "an attempt to suit the Roman Catholic service" are not quite accurate as given without qualification. They occur within a splendid part of *The Oxford History of Music* and would be literally true if they declared this music to have *become* material for the concert room and to have *seemed* to Roman Catholics of the time to be the most acceptable settings of psalms since Benedetto Marcello's *Fifty Psalms* for chorus and orchestra, published 1724–1726. In fact Mendelssohn's church music, apart from his fine organ works and his tributes to Great Britain, were first intended for services held either in the Prussian Court Chapel, in St. Hedwig's Cathedral, Berlin, or in St. Thomas's Church, Leipzig. He must often have wished that Lutheranism had not undergone so drastic a change in its musical worship as it did during the lives of Bach and Handel (see comments on pp. 55ff) losing both the ceremonious liturgy which suggested solemn, professional music and also a reasonably uniform order throughout protestant Germany such as had been secured in England by the enforcement of statutory services as printed in the Book of Common Prayer. Lutheranism allowed local service books; in its days of high orthodoxy mass and vespers had followed a generally accepted order but after the triumph of the Pietists services were dominated by the local pastors.

It was precisely a wish for uniform worship on the part of Friedrich Wilhelm IV of Prussia (1795–1861) which led that mystically inclined but mentally unstable monarch to do in the name of Luther what Luther had wisely not done—enforce orders of service throughout districts under his sway. This act could not create a desire for other music than hymns once the older traditions had been forgotten for nearly a century. The singing of *Der Tod Jesu*, a solid and somewhat sentimental work by C. H. Graun (1704–1759), kapellmeister to Frederick the Great, was a favourite Passiontide extra and has remained so, corresponding in popularity with Stainer's *The Crucifixion*, but this and the increasing popularity of organ recitals and so-called "services" of sacred music[1] by choral societies and orchestras do not constitute any new musical vitality within

---

[1] Honest folk deplore such "services". If our opinions are genuinely Puritan then we have no right to listen to organ voluntaries at public worship. If they are not, we may deplore the utter transformation of a church into a concert hall as at a Three Choirs Festival, but we have no objection to the use of a church for good music, sacred or concert. Why not then omit the hypocrisy of prayers and the suggestion that we have engaged for £100 or so a professional singer to help our "service"? This year Jews, Hindus and other non-Christians whom I teach have complained that they would love to join in concerts of Christmas music—fifteenth century carols, the Schütz *Christmas Story*, other carols—in what are really concerts organized by the colleges in Durham University. Yet those responsible continue to hold "Carol services" under anglican chaplains three weeks before Christmas. For genuine Christians the holding of Christmas services when Advent has just begun is objectionable; for others the exclusion of non-Christians from musical activities which all might enjoy is equally objectionable, being both snobbish and childishly unneighbourly. On the last occasion which forced me to witness one of these carol "services" I was only too aware of the uncharitable intention, for the affair was plainly cherished as a means of establishing the relative status of participants. The carols were separated by lessons by readers of ascending rank, beginning with a Christian college servant and ascending to the agnostic Master, who was pokered to the lectern and was arrayed in a gorgeous convocation gown with something like the signs of the zodiac embroidered on his backside. What is objectionable in a concert or recital of sacred music?

the Lutheran church. This matter is dealt with in a later chapter. It will suffice here to say that the prime movers in the nineteenth century restoration of old music, especially that of Palestrina and that of Bach, were the Germans, including Protestants who responded to the demands of the Prussian court—J. A. Spitta, Rochus von Liliencron, Mendelssohn and Brahms.

Today we should be shocked, perhaps, if served with Mendelssohn's version of the *St. Matthew Passion*, but at least Mendelssohn did not present his audience with something unloved, a museum exhibit performed with no other resources or expression than were marked on holographs. Any liberties— cuts, insertions, re-scorings—were made to commend the work; it was romanticised, and possibly the only creditable effect the romantic movement had upon protestant church music for choirs was its inspiring of revival of older music. I cannot agree that either Mendelssohn or Brahms lost personality or produced archaic pastiche in most of those compositions which pay tribute to their culture as well as their natural genius. Consider one of Mendelssohn's choral pieces known to English church choirs except where prejudice has denied the familiarity. Originally a recitative, trio and chorus from the unfinished oratorio *Christus*, the Epiphany anthem "Say where is he born the King of Judaea?" is sometimes named "There shall a star from Jacob come forth" after its final chorus. The opening treble recitative "When Jesus was born in Bethlehem" and the following trio for tenor and two basses (representing the Magi) are Mendelssohnian yet in symbolism and texture point to many a Bach cantata, as does also the final chorus which culminates in the chorale *Wie schön leuchtet der Morgenstern*. (Bach associated this chorale not with Epiphany but the Feast of the Annunciation.) Mendelssohn's Psalms also reveal the influence of Bach, and it is high time that those with full orchestra—31, 42, 98 and 115—were back in favour with choral societies and given splendid broadcast performances and recordings. Not to know them is to have an incomplete conception of Mendelssohn's stature. Organists will agree that this might be said of his best fugues and sonatas for organ.

LISZT

Franz Liszt, 1811–1886, did launch a new style in church music, and that with a vengeance. The complete romantic, he launched a style which remained very much his own, whatever effect his example had upon other individualists and nationalists, for instance Janacek. In 1834 Liszt wrote

> It is necessary to invoke a new church music which for lack of another epithet we may call humanitarian . . . It should combine the theatre with the church and be at the same time holy and dramatic, simple and splendid, earnest and ceremonious, restful and stormy . . . It will be the *fiat lux* of art.

What this verbiage means let him who knows tell us. It is quoted only as proof that this devout and generous man had sincere ideals in church music. Modern churchmen, living after official condemnation of theatrical church music, need reminding that Liszt was an ardent Catholic, destined to take Holy Orders and to end his days in cloistered meditation. Furthermore his faith had fruit in goodness. We hear too much about his fine ladies—the amours that complete the romantic personality—and too little about his lavish giving to the poor, his patronage of the struggling artist (not just musician) and his unselfish campaigning for and "production" of other composers and performers. He happened to be enthusiastic about plainchant—albeit in corrupt forms, and not for scholarly reasons but because of its romantic evocations of the past. In his first mass of 1884, for men's voices and organ, and in his *Missa choralis* of 1865, originally *a cappella*, Liszt made much use of "gregorian" and modal features. The broadcasting of all his choral music, covering many programmes, revealed much that was unexpectedly restrained and much in contrapuntal texture that cost some abnegation of personality, yet we find similar features in his best secular music—the piano sonata, the *Faust Symphony*, *Prometheus*, etc. His ideals of church music were plainly in conflict, but romantic vitality came uppermost as in Berlioz, one of his heroes. Consequently, whether we like them or not, his two most interesting and characteristic masses are those demanding the largest orchestral and vocal resources —the *Graner Festmesse* of 1855, composed for the dedication of a basilica at Gran, seat of the Hungarian cardinal, and the *Hungarian Coronation Mass* of 1867.

The later of these is the shorter and less flamboyantly dramatic, but it proclaims romantic belief in freedom of expression by its Magyar gipsy rhythms, such as we meet in the composer's Hungarian Rhapsodies (Ex. 4). Even so, we meet in the *Mass for Gran* a more extreme departure from the ideal of Cecilian societies. Influenced by his championship of Wagner's dramas, which he conducted at Weimar, Liszt sought the psychological effect of recurrent musical motives. They could be a liability, for his thematic alliances between *Christe eleison* and *Sanctus*, *Gloria* and *Et resurrexit* are not justifiable as connecting sacred ideas; but they may have another justification. Wagner used motives to integrate structures that might sprawl; rather than produce incoherent music he would make the act of a music drama into a vast symphony and if at any point the voices could not otherwise join the symphony they would have to sing repeated notes or have whatever "line" suited the harmony and rhythm already fixed by the orchestra. Recurrent motives are almost essential to admirable composition of more than a few bars, and most inferior choir music is insufficiently thematic, so that beautiful settings of single phrases are wasted upon pieces which merely "go on"; that is why Stanford's arrival made a significant change in anglican choir music. Liszt was not at fault *because* he applied to church music the convincing structural methods of secular music (especially since his favourite recurrent ideas were church intonations), but because he had faults as a composer, secular or sacred. One was his habit of repetition without variation or

B

expansion, repetition of a rhetorical gesture, attitudinising where invention and development were urgent; another was

Ex. 5

the occasional lame or crude transformation of a theme or the choice for transformation of a theme which was too little a theme and too much an idea wanted for itself, untransformed, at a certain stage in a work. Let it be said at once, however, that the achievements of this great man far outnumbered his faults, even purely as a composer in the narrowest sense of the designation. The *Mass for Gran* belongs to its age, and I do not quarrel with those who think it should never be heard in conjunction with an actual mass; but I also think that those who are unwilling to hear it at a concert as a notable piece of sacred romantic music have much to learn. Here I quote only two extracts (Ex. 5), first the very opening which, in its stealthy shift from tonality shows what Liszt learnt from the classical approach to long movements, then the opening of *Gloria* which gives us a dramatic evocation of the angelic *Gloria in excelsis* at the first Christmas.

BRAHMS

In 1855, soon after the *Mass for Gran,* Liszt produced the most perfervid of his Psalms—Psalm 13 for chorus, orchestra, and a tenor solo in which, he said, he had "allowed *myself* to sing, and allowed the bodily presence of King David to inspire me". This declaration is worthy of Berlioz. Liszt reissued this Psalm in 1865 to the German words of Luther's translation, and Parry notes that Brahms was engaged upon the same words in his Op. 27

> at about the same time. Party strife was then at its height, and the two versions may be taken to represent the conflicting ideals of style under which German musicians ranged themselves in hostile camps—*Zukunftsmusik* on the one side, uncompromising classicism on the other.

In the remarks that follow Parry is less than fair to Liszt, and although Brahms's deliberately reticent setting (for three-part women's voices with organ) is in strong contrast with Liszt's passionately dramatic setting, it is not an example of "uncompromising classicism", nor is any fine work by Brahms, who cunningly uses emotional restraint in one part of a work to emphasise the glowing romantic warmth in another. (An example of this is the "Tragic Overture", wherein a grey, somewhat severe contrapuntal idea is developed until it cedes to rapturous lyricism.) The truth is that Brahms's motets and sacred part songs belong, with some of Mendelssohn's church works, to that north German romantic school which discovered certain ideals in Bach and Bach's predecessors.

Johannes Brahms, 1833–1897, was agnostic, much preoccupied with the mysteries of death and suffering, and a constant reader of Luther's Bible. Despite his devotion to choir music, and his direction of choirs at Detmold and Hamburg for which he composed religious pieces, we cannot easily speak of his church music; instead we must say that churches are greatly indebted to him and glad to use as church music what was not composed as such. His eleven chorale preludes, his wonderful fugue in A flat minor and his less important prelude and fugue in G minor constitute the most admirable one-man treasury of organ music since Bach's, and perhaps the finest evidence of Bach study; and few pieces for choirs are more worth impressing into church use on appropriate occasions than Brahms's motets and his part songs to scriptural texts or to the words of chorales. A pity that we so rarely hear in churches any other music by Brahms than items from *A German Requiem*, such as "How lovely are thy dwellings" and "Ye who now sorrow", along with the pleasant but insubstantial *Marienlieder* at Christmas or on Mary feasts. Some of the best motets and part songs from Op. 29, 74 and 110 are inexpensively available translated into English by the Rev. G. H. Palmer (Lengnick). True, they expose the inferiority of most English anthems, yet Stanford's splendid motets—only one of which is widely used, and that *ad nauseam*—were surely inspired by Brahms's. Perhaps choirmasters are dismayed at the time necessary for their rehearsal, for much work went into their composing and much is demanded for their proper performance; these are not works to keep in service lists and merely brush up during part of a single rehearsal.

Their counterpoint is virtuosic in its freedom. Any trained musician can fulfil the traditional shapes of counterpoint—canti fermi, canons, stretti and so on—demonstrating craftsmanship but not necessarily artistic expression. Brahms, like Purcell and Bach, but very few others, practised until he could use device without fulfilling a prescribed mould or forcing words to melodies and harmonies that were not recognisably his own. We see in Ex. 6A his hinting at canon—and what fifth-rate composer could not complete the canon and produce dull music? We see in Ex. 6B chromatics that belong to his own century, and what silly little fashion follower will find them sugary or the texture anything but vastly superior to most supplied for church consumption since? This book will not have been entirely useless if it induces a few readers to make their first acquaintance with this glorious *Warum?* (Wherefore hath the light been given?) and its companion motet of Op. 74, "O Saviour let the skies be riven"—a cumulative series of chorale treatments comparable with Bach's *Jesu meine Freude*.[1] Ex. 6 shows a few openings of its sections. I apologise for not knowing yet if the chorale is Brahms's own. I have not met it elsewhere and am surprised that it has not found a place in our hymn books.

In order to notice regional and idealistic contrasts among the greater composers I shall wilfully abandon chronological order at this point and turn to the Gallican church (for safety spelt with capital and small initial letters!) which we shall see undergoing the onset of the romantic movement but almost totally unaffected by the isolated figure of Berlioz. If Berlioz be left out, that movement showed far less effect upon French music than upon French literature until after the middle of the century, for the music most venerated by the romantic poets, painters and novelists of Paris was that of foreigners they adopted —first Liszt but then, above all, Chopin, a Pole of French ancestry who left no church music. Moreover two of the most

---

[1] And more useful than Bach's great work during services because it is so much shorter and needs only four vocal parts.

considerable church composers of Paris, Cherubini and Rossini, were not only Italians but artists who belonged in style and approach to the older generations, the classical school of the eighteenth century; but since their best church music came

Ex. 6

from them late in their lives we shall return to them after we have taken our survey forward to the years when these works appeared.

GOUNOD

In the year when Liszt produced his *Mass for Gran*, Charles Gounod, 1818–1893, wrote the best known of his fifteen masses, the *Messe solonelle de Ste. Cécile*. The title suggests sympathies with the idealists, and Gounod was a particularly devout churchman who felt guilty for becoming a successful theatre composer and stifling a vocation to the priesthood. Yet the romantic spirit led him to tamper with his text in a way expressly forbidden by the Vatican. Between the clauses of *Agnus Dei* he inserted a solo passage to the words *Domine, non sum dignus*, an interpolation which he thought justified because it is said by the priest just before administering Holy Communion.[1] At *Dona nobis pacem* there is another romantic touch; the orchestra is silent and the voices finish alone. We do not meet in French church music the violent and grandiosely dramatic manifestations of romanticism which we find in Liszt's, but the lyricism which gave new charm to French theatre music when reaction set in against the "Grand Opera" of Spontini and Meyerbeer. There is nothing turgid or Napoleonic about the church music of Gounod, Guilmant, Saint-Saëns, Dubois and Edgar Tinel. The last mentioned was a Belgian associated with Mechlin, and his church music was extremely popular both in France and England. Like the others he was interested in the plainsong revival and in the reform of church music, but he was also, like them, at his best in songs and operas. In French music we are less troubled by reminders of grand stage settings than by reminders of intimately pathetic scenes in operas like *Mireille* (Gounod), *Louise* (Charpentier), *Thaïs* (Massenet) and *Samson et Dalila* (Saint-Saëns). Even the classically neat Saint-Saëns in the excellent mass which we once sang to English as "Saint-Saëns in G minor" sometimes reveals "the little Massenet" which Debussy declared to be in every one of his musical contemporaries and seniors. We are also reminded of salon pieces and songs. (Incidentally let any man who doubts Gounod's greatness play and sing his magnificent songs.) Massenet's vein of luxurious tearfulness is much to the fore in French Benediction and Marian hymns, now rarely heard in city churches, and still more in the *voix celestes* of Élevations, Prières, Communions and other organ pieces which supplemented or replaced the singing of the Proper. (When Widor was at St. Sulpice a midday Low Mass drew greater congregations than the 10 o'clock

---

[1] The composer's actual comments are given in Camille Bellaigue's *Gounod*, Paris, 1919.

High Mass at which seminarists sang chant according to Solesmes principles; at noon there was no singing but organiacs might enjoy M. Widor's pieces and extemporisations.)

FAURÉ

The French composers just mentioned were better *composers* than Berlioz and Liszt though less important as artists. Gounod was among the most admirable of composers, perhaps nowhere more so in church music than in the Requiem of 1893. He died while composing this work, almost literally pen in hand. Merely to play the vocal score, with its subtle progressions unparalleled by German composers, is to think "How much Fauré owed to this!", until one discovers that Fauré's own noble Requiem had been composed six years previously and had undoubtedly influenced Gounod's. No more sensitive musician had composed since Mozart. The very limitations of Gounod and Massenet made them idiomatic and seemingly national, and if they themselves had produced no enduring music their work would have been worth while because it was absorbed and excelled by Gabriel Fauré, 1845–1924. Rarely did Fauré use his talents more wonderfully than in the exquisite *Requiem* begun in 1886 and finished two years later. It is church music, for it has often been used for commemoratory services and its effect in the concert hall is so to transport our minds from secular to sacred circumstances that we wish applause were forbidden. It was prompted partly by a request from the *Société nationale* (founded to encourage French art under the Third Republic) and partly by his own bereavement of beloved parents. It was first used for an All Souls Day at the Madeleine.

The greatness of Fauré is not apparent to those who dislike artists who subtly reserve their power and scorn forensic rhetoric; Fauré is almost over-civilised in his willingness to let style hold expression in rein. A journalist recently said that he had gone one Saturday from a performance of Brahms's

"Great Requiem" to one of Fauré's "Little Requiem". Though a devoted Brahmin as well as an ardent Wagnerite I must protest, and I am supported by all professional musicians of my acquaintance. The great *Requiem* is not Brahms's but Fauré's, despite Brahms's much larger array of voices and instruments. It is no foolish disparagement of Beethoven, Brahms or any other German-speaking first-rank composer, to declare that though he may have been (in Brahms's case certainly was) an artist of greater range than Fauré he has not excelled Fauré within his wilful limits. *A German Requiem* is an admirable suite of choral and solo cantatas and would remain so if we omitted some and added others. We might, for instance, add *A Song of Destiny* or the *Alto Rhapsody* and still have an even bigger *German Requiem* neither more nor less integral. Brahms's work is nearly all great music but its items are not "all parts of one stupendous whole". Now although I have heard Fauré's *Sanctus* and *Agnus* detached from the complete *Requiem* they certainly are parts of a wonderful whole—one shuns the Popian epithet because of Fauré's distaste for anything stupendous. No composer of his stature was so reticent, so rarely wrote "*ff*", so wholly shunned the explosive.

Much of this masterpiece is devoutly consolatory, and Fauré availed himself of the permissive substitution of the responsory *Libera me* for the sequence *Dies irae*, but he served here no more soothing syrup. In many passages this music is disturbing, despite the hypnotic loveliness of its melody, harmony and texture. No composer should set the catholic requiem if, like Brahms, he wishes to evade the expression of fear and awe and replace it with sentiments of elegiac penitence. From the very opening of the Fauré requiem there is an uncanny musical equivalent of *pompes funèbres* partly evoked by the instrumentation. During most of the work violins and upper woodwind instruments are not used, the tone of the uppermost line being that of violas (Ex. 7A). Restraint and subtlety suggest dread in a way impossible by Beethovenian rhetoric or the theatrical eloquence of Berlioz and Liszt. We may be thrilled by Verdi's apocalyptic trumpets but we enjoy them as we do a medieval painting; however brilliant the technique the conception is naïve. But when (in *Libera me*) Fauré reaches the words

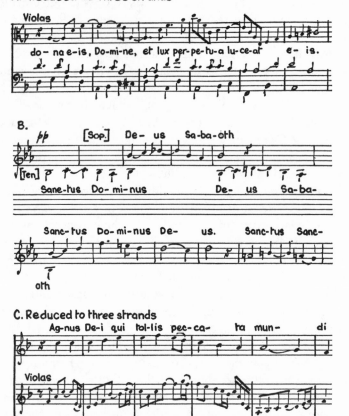

Ex. 7

"Dies irae, dies illa, dies magna et amara valde" he is too sophisticated to use a single trumpet; his symbolism is done with the persistent monotone horn call in octaves, but its

effect is terrifying. (It is actually marked "*f*"!) Previously there
has been a notable horn entry, one of the most wonderful in
all music because of its musical context; it is the mere sounding
of a fifth just before "Osanna in excelsis". A mere skeleton of
the opening of the *Sanctus* (Ex. 7B) serves to show the eloquence
of Fauré's unemphatic wit—wit being the quality dependent
upon past mastery of a language and medium as well as perfect
timing of vocabulary. It is here masked by superficial simplicity
yet produces a hypnotic effect rare in church music except in
the repeated cadences of responsory chant.

Still more remarkable is the fact that this work can reveal its
solemnity and its astringent sensuousness without metro-
politan performers. Indeed the conductor or singer who
imposes upon it his or her vigorous "interpretation", derived
from Italian coloratura or Beethovenian symphony, instead of
accepting Fauré's undemonstrative intensity will spoil music
that casts its spell when faithfully performed by a provincial
choir, a small organ and a few local instrumentalists who
rehearse to competence. Not a note is out of place even in the
radiant not-quite-Gounodian finale, though at first hearing one
marvels how this urbane composer, with artful suggestion of
artlessness, produces a child-like vision of everlasting happiness.
Alas that Fauré composed so little church music! Except the
early *Messe basse* for female voices and organ, his other church
pieces are unimportant offertories and Benediction hymns
which too often sound as if they could be made into nocturnes
or impromptus for piano.

ROSSINI

Gioacchino Rossini, 1792–1868, frequently lived in Paris during
his years of opera composition and he settled there in middle
age. His church music is not classifiable with that of Frenchmen. Not even Gounod, let alone Fauré, gives indication in
his music that the most idolised musician of the nineteenth
century ever lived in the same city as himself. At least we know

where we are with Rossini, for his attitude to the liturgy belongs to the century in which he was born. He meant no irreverence by his rum-ti-tum accompaniments; he simply felt it his duty to do his professional best in church as in theatre, avoiding such idioms as pattering repeated notes that belonged obviously to opera buffa. His *Stabat Mater* of 1832 was trounced by Heine and Wagner; given opportunity they would no doubt have trounced his *Petite Messe solonelle* of 1863, for Rossini called it "the last mortal sin of my old age". A non-aristocratic society can be harsh towards artists who jest about their work, for they suggest that they do not flatter the listener by disturbing their souls for him. The title *Petite Messe* for a vast and magnificent affair, was thought at first to be a sally at composers like Gounod who called works *Grandes Messes solonelles* (*de Pâques, de Pentecôte,* and so on) but in fact this was Rossini's shame-faced piety, for there followed a dedication to "Dear God . . . Have I composed music that is sacred or only sacred music? I was born to compose opera, comic opera, well Thou knowest. Then by Thou praised and grant me entry to Paradise". The Cecilians would have had every right to condemn Rossini's work provided that they had also condemned the church music of Haydn, Mozart, Beethoven and Schubert. As music Rossini's *Messe solonelle* is more splendid than any work of that designation emanating from Paris.

CHERUBINI

To be logical the two egregious Germans should have condemned the church music of Rossini's senior, Luigi Cherubini, 1760–1842, a Florentine who lived in Paris from 1788. After Napoleon's concordat with the church he wrote much church music and was appointed music director of the chapel royal after Napoleon's downfall. He composed the Mass for the coronation of Charles X, but his two best pieces of church music are his Mass in F for the consecration of the church at Chimay and his C minor Requiem. Their dignity and restraint do not come from Cecilian beliefs that church music should differ in style from secular but from the fact that all his music is characterised by the careful fashioning of total shapes, not love of passing effect. Like Gluck in his later operas, Cherubini can sometimes be oppressively dignified and staid, yet Beethoven thought him the most admirable of his contemporaries and specially admired *Les deux journées*.[1] Cherubini's art was too classical to be popular in the age of Rossini and Boieldieu, and Cherubini was held in honour chiefly as Director of the Conservatoire and therefore the trainer, in person or by textbook, of almost all French musicians. He was the leading demonstrator of counterpoint, orchestration and formal composition. His mastery of counterpoint and his expert knowledge of voices ensured that his church music nowhere fell below a fine level; like much in his operas, even the magnificent *Medea* which was among Brahms's favourite scores, Cherubini's church music often seems unimpassioned. It is a pity that I cannot easily supply at least a quotation from his C minor Requiem, but a quotation short enough to suit this book could not show the two most admirable qualities: (1) the fine paragraphs in which counterpoint and modulation are planned on a big scale, (2) the splendid orchestral accompaniment to choruses which can be fully appreciated only in full score.

VERDI

As he approached old age the most passionate and forceful of Italian opera composers, Giuseppe Verdi, 1813–1901, had come to command Cherubini's contrapuntal skill, but Verdi's church music is surely not intended for liturgical worship. It was Verdi himself who proposed in 1868 to the publisher Ricordi that several Italian composers might contribute to a Requiem in honour of Rossini; it was to be performed annually

[1] A rescue opera that influenced Beethoven's *Fidelio*. Beethoven sought Cherubini's advice after the failure of *Lenore*, the first version of *Fidelio*. What is more, he followed it!

in the large basilica of St. Petronio in Bologna, famous for its association with great string players and trumpeters in the seventeenth and early eighteenth centuries, on each anniversary of Rossini's death. Only the *Libera me* has survived, being now part of Verdi's great Requiem for Manzoni who died in 1873. Manzoni was a devout poet, dramatist and novelist whose historical story *I promessi sposi* became known in translations throughout Europe. I do not wish to comment here upon Verdi's *Requiem*, except to say that it is among those supreme works of genius which seem to gather features from all comparable works preceding it for almost a century; yet it includes felicitous unorthodoxy. We also hear in the concert room one or two of Verdi's other brilliant "church" compositions, the *Quattro Pezzi Sacri*, which were also written in his last years. Nobody else has presented *Stabat Mater* and *Te Deum* more powerfully in such brief settings, and these two of the four pieces are naturally the most frequently heard. Their orchestral and vocal brilliance commends them for concerts. The other two are for voices only. The women's voices setting of Dante's *Laudi alla Verginé Maria* is exquisite and immediately appealing, but the four-voice *Ave Maria* uses one of those enigmatic scales with which Liszt experimented. It forms a cantus firmus for each voice in turn, the bass first, while the others supply counterpoint. The piece is not easy to sing and not wholly convincing as a treatment of those words.

BRUCKNER

At the very end of the chapter we reach the greatest church composer of the romantic century, Anton Bruckner, 1824–1896. If this description is misapplied, who is Bruckner's rival?[1] The greatest church composer must be he who composed the most *first-rank* music actually *for church use*, and some part of this qualification cuts out every composer previously discussed.

[1] Not Dvořák, whose pretty D major mass and Birmingham Festival *Te Deum* do not earn him a place in this chapter.

Until recently we were not familiar with more than two of Bruckner's symphonies, though in Vienna all of them came almost as frequently in programmes as did some of the greater classical symphonies. This fact need not make us proud of Vienna and ashamed of London. The Viennese repertory is more provincial than most. Whatever the just complaints of British musicians and music-lovers (I have voiced or signed several) the B.B.C. and other London music givers cover a far wider historical and geographical repertory than the music givers of Vienna. Inspecting a whole season's opera, concert and radio programmes I wondered if the Viennese public knew a single work by Bartok, Blacher, Sibelius, Roussel, Fauré, to say nothing of British and American or *avant garde* composers. I saw nothing advertised by their own Alban Berg. Vienna's citizens like music in their own language. They feel cosy with the classical symphonists and their successors, Strauss, Mahler and Bruckner, and a few other German-speaking masters. As Bruckner's are the longest of their symphonies they provide a splendid moneysworth and a big, warm orchestra. Viennese enthusiasm does not necessarily indicate musical perception, but our own neglect of Bruckner certainly does indicate our lack of perception. Perhaps we are put off by some of Bruckner's champions. When an artist has not received his due, his cause is not helped by the assertion that his work is "as good as" someone else's. Scarlatti's harpsichord pieces are *not* as good as Bach's, but neither are Bach's as good as Scarlatti's. Each treasury is pricelessly good and each is *sui generis*, and this is true of the symphonies of Brahms and Bruckner, foolishly set up as rivals by the Wagnerite faction. Bruckner was said to prove that Wagnerian technique could make symphonies. No proof was needed. For the first movement play the second act of *The Valkyrie*, or *Siegfried's Journey down the Rhine*, for slow movement play *Forest Murmurs* or the Tristan *Liebesträume*, for scherzo the *Ride of the Valkyries*, etc. But why even this composite proof? What intelligent musician fails to hear in every act of *The Ring* the unfolding of a symphony? Bruckner, the shy organist, more happy with his confessor than the sophisticated twaddlers of foyers, found himself ill at ease as the hero of a faction. He wanted to honour Wagner just as he honoured Schubert, Beethoven, Bach and Palestrina; for though he was socially gauche and naïve let there be no mistake about his *musical* intelligence or his *musical* scholarship.

Because Bruckner was peasant-like in appearance, gauche in "society" (the economist's name for sheep and the snob's for fools), hesitant or naïvely voluble in conversation, awkward in his dealings with women yet longing for the married state which he never attained, it is customary to say "Poor Bruckner!" He elicited pity especially during his later years of high professional status and recognition as an artist, for he shrank from honour. He suffered from nervous breakdowns and one biography even describes his (non-violent) last illness as "religious mania". Would it have gone so far if he had been a monk or priest? If I die in mental or nervous prostration and babble of fields and hedgerows, streams, my chrysanthemums and the wild birds over which I sentimentalise, will it be said that I suffer from "nature mania"? It happens that these things fill my fancy when I am composing myself to sleep and are more often in my mind than music or religion, the practices of which I tend to accept as I do meals and the duties of a livelihood. Why should Bruckner's uppermost desires and comforts be more morbid than mine? (Mine certainly *are* morbid for they include a desire for the painless decimation of the population in order that "development" and vehicles shall not ruin more of the countryside.) The "inner" Bruckner cannot have been pitiable, for his music belies the supposition. He was probably happier than most of us with the comforts and symbolism of his religion (in its sumptuous yet peasant-appealing Austrian forms) and he was also happy with his succession of appreciative employers.

Bruckner was an orphan chorister with the St. Florian monks, at whose school he had excellent teachers. After going to a teacher's training college and serving in several village schools he went back to St. Florian as organist in that magnificent baroque chapel. Then, as cathedral organist at Linz, he no longer needed to supplement his income with the schoolmaster's duties which were probably as uncongenial to him as to Schubert. He could hear music in Vienna and study with the most intelligent of contrapuntists, Simon Sechter, and with the Linz kapellmeister, Otto Kitzler, whose tutorings and opera performances revealed the marvel of Wagner. (He did not actually meet Wagner until the Munich performance of *Tristan* in 1865.) He was offered the Conservatory and University appointments at Vienna in 1868 and also made organist at the imperial chapel. He was free to visit various German and foreign cities for performances of his symphonies and to give recitals. (He was greatly admired in London for his playing and extemporisation, and he had five concerts to himself at the Crystal Palace). If it had not been for the *Wagner Verein* he would not have been worried by the gibes of Hanslick and the Brahmins, but surely these did not shake the reclusive joy of his study, his organ loft, his frequent devotions in church! His music tells of glory and gazing at glory—the very solid and highly coloured glory of those baroque monastic churches of the Danube and of Wagner's Valhalla. Even the ponderous struggling to glory brings no really bleak or agonised expression, and we are never taken by Bruckner into the unearthly regions of Beethoven's last quartets.

Bruckner knew more about plainchant and polyphony than the Cecilians, whose opinions on his works concerned him anxiously. He was attracted to the more sombre work of Victoria and had an unexplained fondness for Gallus. Baroque counterpoint was part of his equipment even before the studies with Sechter for he had regularly participated from childhood in music by Vinci, Lotti, Leo, Legrenzi, Caldara and Carissimi—all composers favoured on ferial days as well as during Advent and Lent. He knew Bach well chiefly through his organ and keyboard works, but except in his academic studies he did not, like the Cecilians, compose parodistic archaisms; the technique of polyphonists and baroque contra-puntists fertilised his more direct stylistic inheritance as an Austrian, that from Schubert and Schubert's smaller con-temporaries and successors. If Bruckner had died at forty he would hardly be counted a great or unique artist, but his many masses and other church pieces would have been distinguished from most Viennese *Kapellmeistermusik* by their dignified yet interesting textures, and by a demand upon performers which could not easily be met outside the greater churches of Austria and Bavaria. The implications of the splendid fugue subject shown at Ex. 8 would not be fulfilled by most church choirs of Italy, France or England.[1]

Bruckner matured late. He became a significant artist in his forties and the catalyst in his development was Wagner. Most composers indebted to Wagner have been overwhelmed by one particular drama, *Tristan and Isolde*, but the Wagnerian music that Bruckner absorbed into his unique expression came from the *Ring* dramas with their primarily triadic rather than chromatic harmony. What made Bruckner a symphonist is what made Sibelius one—the huge paragraphing which is often dependent upon a slow rate of harmonic change. It would be intolerably ponderous if texture were not enlivened by (*a*) polyphony, (*b*) colour, (*c*) the sense of forward trend. In Bruckner this latter becomes a crescendo (not simply of dynamics) like the swelling of an organ, nearly always symbolis-ing the expectation of glory. We are not here concerned with his Viennese scherzos which commended him to us before we understood the rest of his personality. Rather let us consider his slow movements, which ponderously evolve in the model of the adagio in Beethoven's Ninth—with this difference, that they reach codas wherein tubas and trombones give an organ-like texture to full orchestral glory. The inspiration came from

[1] One or two quite attractive Bruckner church pieces are available in this country. Just the right length for unaccompanied anthem or motet is *Christus factus est* with English text *Christ was born for our salvation* published by Curwen. The piece is in four strands throughout with no "divided" voices, and its effect is splendid.

such passages as the entry of the gods into Valhalla or the climax of Siegfried's exultant journeys: the slow approach, the

Ex. 8

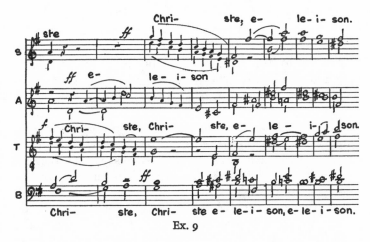

Ex. 9

promise of vast scale, was shown in music which must surely never be imitated, for an imitation of the prelude to *Rheingold* would be intolerable.

Bruckner's finest church works are the Mass in D minor of 1864, the Mass in E minor of 1866, the *Grosse Messe* in F minor of 1876 (as its title suggests, the longest) the *Te Deum* of 1884 and the *Psalm CL* of 1892. All these are for full orchestra and choir with soloists except the Mass in E minor, which owes more to Cecilian ideals,[1] being for eight-part chorus and fifteen wind instruments (four horns and three trombones with a pair of oboes, clarinets, bassoons and trumpets) and thus secures the glory without soloists and with more recourse to counterpoint. It is almost ridiculous to quote from works on the scale of Bruckner's symphonies or masses unless one can quote several pages and show the groping tread to glory; yet at Ex. 9 I have wilfully chosen a longish extract from the vocal parts alone in the very one of the great Bruckner masses (the E minor) which gains its power by the apparent restriction of orchestral colour and vocal homophony. Without the organ and wind instruments this vocal texture suggests the Wagnerian motivic growth as well as the crescendo and climax of a Bruckner symphony.

Fortunately Bruckner's splendid *Te Deum* is becoming a favourite choral work here and needs no comment, but it is worth quoting from the late Dr. H. C. Colles, not a musician predisposed to like either Bruckner or his liturgical tradition, some remarks he made in the *Oxford History of Music* about Bruckner's most ambitious church work:

> In the *Grosse Messe* in F minor, a work of larger scope and freer expression than the earlier masses, Bruckner is seen at his best. . . . His church music as a whole, considered as the outcome of his national tradition, appears to give him a higher place as a composer than that to which his symphonies entitle him. It is true that it will not readily bear transplantation either into the concert room or into the ritual of any other form of Christian worship than that which inspired it. We in England, who have a tradition of church music equally incapable of transplantation,

[1] The modal, unaccompanied motet *Osjusti* of 1879 shows that Bruckner could have beaten the Cecilians in their own field whenever he wished.

should appreciate the value of local art forms within the borders of the Christian Church.

To that tribute one dares to add the observation that "local forms" never yet took a cubit off the stature of a great artist. The J. S. Bach of the local and denominational art forms is now more greatly regarded than the J. S. Bach who, before he became Leipzig Cantor, set out on a less localized career which would have made him purveyor of international art forms such as suites, concertos and sonatas (perhaps operas as well) for princely music rooms.

3

Continental Church Music—1

ADVANCE OR REVIVAL?

I. THE LUTHERAN DECLINE

Sweelinck, Praetorius, Schütz, Scheidt, Schein, Buxtehude and many other composers of vocal and instrumental church music could be invoked to support a claim that, despite the glory of Venice under Giovanni Gabrieli, Monteverdi and Legrenzi, despite the excellence of Leo and Durante, and of several fine musical directors at Vienna, Salzburg or Munich, our finest treasury of seventeenth century church music came from Lutherans. Its jewels are outshone in the eighteenth century by one man and it could further be claimed that, whether its citizens recognized the fact or not, Leipzig from 1723 to 1750 regularly enjoyed the finest church music heard for over a century. Let it not be forgotten that Hamburg, Eisenach and many another centre of the old "high" or orthodox Lutheranism also enjoyed the magnificent choral and instrumental music which was thought proper for its regular eucharistic *Haupgottedienst* and Vespers, to say nothing of its Passions in Holy Week and its cantatas on Sundays and week-day festivals.

It is one thing to hear Bach cantatas or chorale preludes in a centrally heated hall or church, or in one's home, and another to hear them, as did Bach's contemporaries, during a morning service which had become so elaborate that it lasted over four hours on high festivals. All too glib are the musicographers who tell us of the devotion aroused by preludes and variations (not "voluntaries" but "compulsories" played *during* the service) upon "popular" chorales. Oh yes, they *ought* to have been popular, and so they had been for more than a century after

54

Luther, but they were less popular in Bach's time than were the sentimental Pietist hymns. Bach fought to maintain in regular use the Communion or Catechism chorales and the seasonal office hymns or *Detemporelieder*. This was not merely in order that cantatas and organ pieces could be built upon them but because, as a staunch traditionalist and Orthodox Lutheran, he hated Calvinistic trends. Leipzig was the last stronghold of Orthodoxy and its champion was Dr. August Pfeiffer whose "Antimelancholicus" and "Anticalvinismus" Bach managed to buy for his library out of his very slender income. But can we, by repeating the truth that *Vexilla regis* and *Pange lingua* have lasted for centuries and that their words and music are rich and moving beyond those of any later hymns, make them loved by people who think them less rich and moving than "Abide with me" or some Negro spiritual?

We know from a memorandum kept by Rost, the custos or sacristan at St. Thomas's, and from additions by his successor, that until 1776 Leipzig retained the externals of High Mass and sang the Ordinary first to plainchant in Latin, *Kyrie* and *Gloria* being "figural" or choral except in penitential seasons, and then repeated them to Luther's vernacular chorale settings—*Allein Gott in der Höh sei Ehr, Wir glauben all in einen Gott* etc. The elaborate choral and instrumental *Konzert, Hauptmusik* or *Stuck* (which we call the Cantata) was replaced by the *Motett* in Advent and Lent. The sacristan's *aide-mémoire* does not tell us how long after Bach's fight against on-coming Pietism the boy choristers and orchestral instruments were retained. While Telemann was at Hamburg the musical elaboration continued and the chief morning service remained eucharistic; but it did not include Latin, which Luther wanted where there were universities or where "it would be good for schoolboys".

All this grandeur and fine music had completely disappeared from German protestant worship (even in court chapels) by 1800. The normal service consisted of said prayers, readings, and long sermon, interspersed with a few slowly sung hymns led by a "cock-and-hen" choir. One inheritance remained— the fine German organs and organ-playing, though it had more scope during the nineteenth century in catholic churches, and almost all the famous German recitalists of the century held appointments under the Roman obedience. We have mentioned Graun's *Der Tod Jesu* as an occasional musical "extra" in the round of protestant music. One of the best among many minor composers whose "extras" were sung occasionally (as are anthems elsewhere), was J. A. Hiller (1728–1804) one of Bach's successors as Cantor at St. Thomas's; but the lack of any urgent call for fine music in the Lutheran church is evident in the diminished implications of the title "Cantor"; it incurred neither the duties nor the stimuli that drew Bach to Leipzig. Hiller was only by sinecure the Leipzig City Cantor; his work was really as organist and music director of St. Thomas (and only St. Thomas), and it demanded no more of him than would such a post at a Scottish kirk in a small town today. Consequently Hiller's main interest was in *Singspiel* at the Leipzig theatres and in his work as a peripatetic conductor of concerts and choral societies in various German cities. Still more significant is the fact that this Lutheran cantor's most ambitious church pieces were a mass and a *Stabat Mater*! It should be mentioned, however, that he also compiled a protestant hymn book which included some of the chorales that had fallen into desuetude.

2. THE PRUSSIAN REVIVAL

We already noticed, however, in our discussion of Mendelssohn (pp. 28ff) that, partly in response to the mystical religiosity of Friedrich Wilhelm IV, partly because of a romantic interest in older German music, there began in the Berlin-Potsdam churches a musical and liturgical revival from the year 1840, that of the King's accession. In Alfred Einstein's words[1] the

[1] *Music in the Romantic Era*, New York, 1947.

Lutheran Church after Bach suffered from "a lack of the creative spirit" which led idealists to "a return to the past" or rather to Bach and Palestrina. "Since the King had a Catholic tinge, and since he considered the ostensibly pure vocal church music of Palestrina the only genuine and authoritative kind, there was in Berlin actually a school that could proclaim that . . . it had brought this music to a state of second flowering."

The last part of this quotation is fully supported by J. A. Spitta (1841–1894), Bach's biographer and the editor of the first collected edition of Schütz's music (almost entirely for the Orthodox Lutheran church as represented in the Dresden court chapel) and of Buxtehude's organ works. His most distinguished successor as an editor and musicologist was Rochus von Liliencron (1820–1912), who had studied theology as well as law, and who became chairman of the Prussian royal commission for the invaluable *Denkmäler* volumes of old music. Liliencron advocated a wholesale reform of Lutheran services which, he hoped, would use the newly edited old music (Senfl, Praetorius, Schütz, Buxtehude, Bach) and inspire new music to follow the church Kalendar in choral, congregational and organ contributions, not with the strictness of the old Orthodoxy but as in the English Church, or indeed the Swedish, for Sweden had not undergone the onslaught of Calvinistic Pietism and, to this day, retains the "High Church" ceremonial and eucharistic morning worship of Orthodox Lutheranism.

Precious little old music (except what lay questionably edited in the Boyce and Arnold volumes) adorned anglican services until the twentieth century. That little was disliked, as we boys rightly disliked what was called *Byrd in D minor* and Merbecke in various minors edited by Stainer. We and worshippers much preferred *Jangler in G*[1] and Stainer's own light-operatic services and anthems, for their styles were understood

---

[1] The innocent reader should not attempt to trace an original edition of this composer's work. It was an invention of Percy Dearmer [Editor].

by our directors. It was their and our opinion that church music before Purcell's lacked expression and had to be drawled. Charles II's tastes were very understandable!

The German scholars and conductors did not make this mistake. Even the cult of Palestrina came from Protestants, largely by impetus from Potsdam and Berlin, and although Giuseppe Baini's biography (almost hagiography) of Palestrina appeared in 1825 the Roman Church was little affected by any "back to Palestrina" idealists until late in the century. We should note that leadership in the movement came from south Germany and Rhineland and was inspired by musicians and clergy who had been in contact with the scholar-idealists of the north. The Prussians could do little with their parish services except in favoured cities, and the fruit of their revivals was tasted more in the concert room or the church "recital" than in actual worship. The south German Catholics had an advantage. Priest-scholars like Haberl and Proske whose performances and editions were centred upon Regensburg (Ratisbon) wanted old music for actual, live worship. For them revival *was* reform, and Regensburg was a good demonstration centre because it contained one of the few continental cathedrals which retained its medieval choral foundation and boys' choir school.

Interest in Bach and Schütz prevented among most German protestant composers the production of pseudo-sixteenth century pieces such as were later to come from Roman Catholics and Anglicans and to launch in church music what corresponds with the Pre-Raphaelite movement in painting, stained-glass and mosaics. As far as I know only one Prussian Cantor became a musical "Nazarene", a German term corresponding with the English "Pre-Raphaelite". He was E. A. Grell, (1800–1886) who was employed by the Prussian court and appointed director of Berlin Cathedral choir in 1839. In him we meet another Lutheran whose finest work is to the Latin ritual, for Grell's masterpiece is an *a cappella* mass of sixteen parts. He regarded with great disfavour the addition of instrumental accompaniment to choir music for the church, thereby unwittingly differing from Palestrina and his advanced contemporaries! On most German composers the effect of the historical revival was wholly admirable, and German pedestrian church musicians produced works of varied texture and polyphonic strength with few parallels in England except the motets of the elder Wesley. Unfortunately few of them are works of sufficient distinction to be known outside Lutheran Germany. There was only one Brahms!

3. HISTORICAL REVIVAL IN CATHOLIC BAVARIA

The effect of scholarship and revival of old music in the Roman Church will be surveyed in the next chapter, but here I emphasise two points I have already mentioned. First, the initiators of historical revival were Germans, not Italians, though many members of the Italian and French hierarchy desired reform and welcomed "reform by revival". Secondly, the Lutherans, however much they liked *hearing* the newly revealed church music of their forebears, especially Bach, and however many of them like to participate in choirs which performed even older music than his, did not regard the newly printed editions of old music as essential to the reform of their liturgy. Only an élite followed the Prussian monarch in that ideal and, to judge by most Lutheran services even in our own century, most German Protestants were content with a liturgy in which music was not an essential but an ornament, as it is in the humbler protestant churches here, established or free. At worship they demanded no more music than hymns and organ playing, with sometimes a choir "extra". The music of Palestrina, Praetorius and so on to Bach and Telemann was pursued *as* music, as a culture, though it might appeal to piety even in a concert hall. German Catholics, on the other hand, put the new copies to immediate use at Mass and Vespers: for them it was in itself the means of a reform in *worship* as well as the inspiration of composers who, wishing for reform, frequently belonged to the "Society of St. Cecilia", originally Bavarian.

4. THE CECILIANS

Cecilian Societies sprang up in other German states and outside Germany. For Roman Catholics, revival and reform were not easy to dissociate.

How urgent was the need for reform in the Roman Church, how inept some of its music was, especially in Italy, during the first half of the nineteenth century, we shall see in the next chapter. It will be enough for the moment to remember that church music was popularly esteemed when it was like the music of the nearest opera house, and that perhaps the most widely esteemed of all actually used musical themes from operas. A spirited instrumental concertato, short and noisy choruses, along with florid solo arias, duets etc.—these were the ingredients of a truly festal service. The combined effort, revival and reform, began timidly between 1830 and 1840, reaching north Italy before Rome. It stemmed from Bavaria, where king Ludwig I (1825–1848), had commissioned Gaspare Ett (1788–1867), to bring to light the liturgical masterpieces of the sixteenth and early seventeenth centuries. Other pioneers of this scholarship were Karl Proske (1794–1861) who issued the volumes called *Musica Divina*, still valuable, and others of the group associated with Ratisbon (at least for publication)—Xavier Witt, founder of the most important of the Societies of St. Cecilia, Franz Xavier Haberl, Michael Haller (the most useful composer of the Ratisbon group), Ignaz Mitterer and Georg Stehle.

The movement extended to :

> *Austria* where the seminary at Salzburg specialised in performances of Palestrina's music under the direction

of Dr. Wilhelm Ambros, an eminent musicological scholar.

Switzerland where the Benedictine Anselm Schubiger (d. 1888) was the author of many influential writings on the reform of church music.

Belgium where the music historian François Fétis (1784–1871) took up the cause of reform.

Spain where the priest-music-director Miguel Eslava, a gifted composer, published several volumes of old Spanish masters.

France where the most important scholarship centred upon the Benedictine Abbey of Solesmes, especially in musical palaeography. The intention of the leading Solesmes scholars was to discover by deciphering manuscripts an authentic interpretation of plainchant performance.

Italy where, as has been suggested, restoration-reform was slow. In the Milan periodical *Musica Sacra* for January–February 1964 Mgr. Caglio traces the desire for restoration back to 1821 in some writings by a priest in Brescia. In 1838 Cardinal Ostini of Jesi sent out an edict against the "abuse of operatic music in church", and it is surprising to learn that the man who persuaded him to do so was Gaspare Spontini (1774–1851), the very composer who produced the most inflatedly "grand" operas for Napoleonic Paris, e.g. *La Vestale*. Spontini happened to be a devout churchman, and he was shocked at the state of Italian music during a short return to his native country. He wrote to the cardinal from Berlin and, receiving a copy of the edict, sent it to Pope Gregory XVI who replied : "Let the diocese of Jesi begin. Others will follow; then I shall act." The Pope formed a commission with Spontini as president. Members included Baini (Palestrina's biographer) and Basili, choirmaster at St. Peter's. They quarrelled, and the commission bore no immediate fruit. Various hierarchical pronouncements on music made between 1824 and 1894 are mentioned in the next chapter, the most important being that of the Patriarch of Venice who became Pope Pius X, author of the famous *motu proprio* of 1903.

5. THE PLAINCHANT REVIVAL

As has so often happened in history, the greatest achievement expected from elsewhere came from France, at first with very little public notice; for the single most important revival of old music, the one to reveal the greatest beauty and to restore performance as well as text, was that of the Benedictine Abbey at Solesmes, a beautiful village on the Sarthe, to the south-west of Le Mans.[1] The community's first abbot in Solesmes (1833), Dom Prosper Guéranger, with his colleague and successor, Dom Joseph Pothier, challenged (*a*) the heavy, hymn-like chanting of plainsong as if it were harmonised music, and indeed the practice of harmonising it note by note, (*b*) the so-called Medicean editions of liturgical chant made at the beginning of the seventeenth century and, because they were "official", espoused by the Ratisbon scholars. Without going into details one may well understand that after this music had for centuries been printed on staves and its oral tradition had been long forgotten, it had lost the free melismatic rhythms of its Byzantine, Hebrew and middle-eastern ancestry. That part of it which was not florid, but set to the recitation of psalms, canticles and such texts as *Credo*, lost its speech-like pace and became treated like the mensural music of the sixteenth and seventeenth centuries. We can imagine its printed appearance and falsified interpretation by comparing plainsong as sung now with the styles of Marbeck's syllabic treatment of the 1549 Prayer Book or the frequent treatment of Schütz's recitatives.

[1] For a period after 1901, in which year the French government confiscated the Solesmes printing press and enforced one of its stupid laws against religious teaching communities, the monks migrated to the Isle of Wight and Desclée of Tournai became their publisher.

Guéranger called the old style "hammered" (martélé) and he engaged in such a spirited opposition of Friedrick Pustet, spokesman for Ratisbon, that Pius X, himself a music-lover who responded to the Solesmes interpretation, referred to him as "Dom Guerroyer"; but this compliment came after his death. Unfortunately Pustet had secured from Pius IX a thirty years' privilege which commended the Ratisbon

Ex. 10

publication of the Medicean versions for general use through-out the church, and Leo XII confirmed it. It was not until 1904, when Pius X was pope and Dom Paul Delatte abbot, that the Solesmes monks were vindicated by the appointment of a commission to prepare what is now called the Vatican Edition. (Naturally there have been further emendations and improvements, but a printing of the improved Vatican Edition with Solesmes marks of interpretation is at present the most widely used form of the chant.)

Guéranger could merely persist in the practical demon-stration of beauty in Solesmes and in communities willing to follow, but he was on firmly demonstrable ground when began photographing codices of the Gregorian period and preparing reproductions for publication. Highly influential were those issued under Pothier—1881 *Les mélodies grégoriennes* and 1883 *Liber gradualis a Geregorio Magno ordinatus*. These at least proved wrong the Medicean underlay of syllables and therefore the falsification of accent. (There is no need to waste time in argument about quantity and accent; a mere glance at harmonised polyphonic music of the late middle ages will show that Latin had become accentual by the influence of vernacular languages in different European countries.) Probably the Solesmes monk whose writings have most influenced musicians of our time is Dom André Mocquereau who began the issue in 1889 of a valuable quarterly which included commentary on photographic facsimiles, *Paléographie musicale*. The fact that many readers may be like Charles Lamb over 'schools' of plainchant interpretation and say to themselves

> Strange all this difference should be
> 'Twixt Tweedledum and Tweedledee

is a testimony to the devoted persistence and triumph of Solesmes. They know other ways of singing plainsong, even if plainsong is used as background or local-colour music in film, play, radio or television performance. Indeed I have had to ask the Ushaw choirmaster to find a Ratisbon book for me so that I can quote at Ex. 10 the contrasts between that and my (Solesmes) *Liber usualis*.

No music is more distinctively Christian, none more powerful in its effect on that part of us which is too deep for tears and passions. It is *not* entirely governed by the words, or it could not include the elaborate neumes and the *jubilus* by which joy was expressed in the early church; nor does it govern the words. The music alone, chanted to a vowel, conveys an effect of timelessness and other-worldliness as does the singing of Hindu sacred music to a prolonged syllable or two of Sanskrit. But in fact plainsong is the perfect marriage of melody, words and worship. By comparison with plainsong any other church music, from the grandest classical masses with orchestra to metrical or harmonised anglican systems of psalmody, seems handicapped in its primary function— that of expressing and conveying specifically Christian praise and prayer with the minimum of irrelevant evocation. Why else should the theatre producer so often put it into requisition? Like the smell of incense or the sight of the large non-ornate crucifix that "hits us" when we enter a Lutheran church, plainsong does all that other church music claims to do without demanding a choir or an instrument. It can solace the solitary singer afield or indoors, it can open heaven for a crowd, and neither the solitary singer nor any member of the crowd need be a better musician than the corncrake. I am tempted to say that the sincerity of our intention in using church music is tested by our willingness to sing simple plainchant, and that we shrink from it simply because it *does* "hit us"; we do not really desire unalloyed the devotion for which public worship is ostensibly held; we want to judge and feel proud of our preacher, our organ, our choir. These are not by worldly standards ignoble sentiments, even if they generate pride in the performers or ourselves! But why, oh why, now that plainsong is no longer thought popish by intelligent people, is not more of it used in *all* churches, and why do not schoolchildren learn some of its great lyrical melodies—*Pange lingua, Urbs beata, Sponsa Christi, Vexilla regis, Veni creator Spiritus, Te ante lucis terminum*—and some simple psalmody as part of their musical culture? I have known undergraduates arrive as music specialists yet have to introduce them to these tremendous classics of their art, not by listening—that method would be worse than useless— but by singing them *fast and heartily* from the little paperback *Plainsong for Schools.*[1] All declare after a mere hour's session that they have had a surprising musical experience which

---

[1] Rushworth and Dreaper, 1s. 3d.

C

they should have had before, and this experience needs no instrument, apparatus or special musical aptitude. If any readers lack it I beg them to take it instead of wasting time reading *about* musical experiences.

I must emphasise the words *fast and heartily*. Plainsong has been falsified and made to seem dull in these islands because we Protestants associate it with religious communities or fine choirs which sing elaborate chant with nuance and careful tone production. Well and good, so long as we do not suppose that a community vocation or a fine voice is essential to the musico-devotional experience without which the chant is mere lecture material. Futhermore we are saddled with an English ritual; much of it is beautiful and so are some of the translations by such men as Cosin, Caswall and Neale which are set to plainsong hymns. Unfortunately the effect and value of plainsong was first perceived by high Anglicans who followed the Tractarians, and they sang it to English as it was sung in mid-nineteenth century to Latin. A pioneer enthusiast, Thomas Helmore, published from 1842 onwards a number of practical manuals—a psalter, a book of office and seasonal hymns, a *Directory of Plainsong* etc.—and also organ accompaniments of the four-part note-for-note variety, which were adopted in many anglo-catholic churches and also in cathedrals for use at "Men only" and "Boys only" services. Then, when the strife about interpretation began to be reflected here, there was adopted by many choirmasters an extraordinary system of performing psalmody and recitative plainchant that was supposed to satisfy any party. Choirs were informed that the chant was disembodied and rhythmless and that every syllable should be popped out with equal force or lack of it; the effect with well-disciplined singers has been likened to that of slow and quiet machine-gun fire.

Do not let us blame Helmore and Neale and the rest; rather let us praise them, for these islands can boast precious little nineteenth century revival of old music to compare with the work of the Prussian, Bavarian and French scholars.

The unjustly maligned Stainer came nearest to them in preparing his *Dictionary of Musical Terms* and his book *Dufay and his Contemporaries* and in discovering a few old English carols. With him must be mentioned the man who appointed him organist at Tenbury in 1856, Ouseley, who himself edited Gibbons's church music "in accordance with ideas then prevailing" as Grove deliciously puts it. The English church, both at cathedral and parish level, was engaged in a revival more absorbing than that consequent upon musicological scholarship, the revival of church and worship as a whole; Ouseley and Stainer played an honourable part in it. Until recently musicians of the Roman Church could say "Take away the Latin and what is the chant?" Now, however, with the adoption in all countries of vernacular for congregational parts of its services, and other parts too, the Roman Church must ask whether the most beautiful and effective of all church music is to be kept only for Latin words or whether protestant errors are to be copied. Protestants are just beginning to recognise either the triviality or the sham archaism of most attempts to ally their eucharistic ritual with any music but the genuine ancient chant. Moreover the Roman Church is at a further disadvantage. She does not inherit the fine cadence of Tudor prose and, to judge by the hideous Italian of the present "official" vernacular of the Ordinary of the Mass, she is in danger of losing precisely the qualities for which her worship has hitherto been enviable. Why could not a catholic poet, such as Tusiani, have been asked to supply a translation of the Mass, and to have consulted musicians while doing so? It remains only to say that I have heard plainsong effectively allied with French words at Taizé and that I have never heard it more heartily sung to English hymn translations than in congregationalist and methodist churches. Of course its ideal association is with the Latin to which it was originally wedded, and if the Roman Church and others would set its more simple forms—the hymns I have mentioned, Masses VIII and XVI, the psalm-tones for the Propers, etc.—to vernacular ritual, surely all but the certifiably weak-minded could all the more enjoy it when they heard it to Latin in cathedral or community, for the complete renunciation of Latin would be a loss deeply felt by Protestants as well as by those Christians who have up to now been its custodians.

4

Continental Church Music—2

CHORAL MUSIC OF THE ROMAN CHURCH

I. STANDARD NINETEENTH CENTURY CUSTOMS

No papal promulgation commands music in all churches of a certain size, nor does any known to me relegate the most important liturgical music in large churches to a choir; yet until recently custom led one to postulate such injunctions. During the nineteenth century music was largely the responsibility of mixed choirs in galleries. Robed boys' choirs behind or in front of the altar, as in Westminster Cathedral and Notre Dame respectively, still represent a minority of their type in the Roman Church. Before describing the wide variety of music and arrangements for music under an authority mistakenly thought to impose uniformity it is worth digressing to make clear two points: (i) Even where mass remains in Latin, present musical usage has changed in many churches since the last war. (ii) The modern traveller, hearing the vernacular used for chorales and hymns where he expects to hear the Proper, or hearing scriptures and prayers read in the vernacular, should not assume that these practices began with a modern liturgical movement. In some countries they are centuries old.

During the nineteenth century, at least in catholic countries, the larger churches were not accustomed to "More or less Low Mass with more or less choir music but certainly with congregational music". Until about 1940 the main Sunday service, held in mid-morning, was either High Mass or, where three priests were not available, a ceremonious near-high celebration called Missa Cantata or Solemn Mass with the same music as High Mass; "cantata" implied "by a choir": a mixture of said and sung was not characteristic of the period we have to study. In Italy and France congregational hymnody rarely had any place in the service, but the people might sing with the choir in the familiar phrygian *Credo* (No. 1 of the *Liber usualis*) in *Pater noster*, or in most of the Ordinary of the Mass if the setting were familiar and easy, for instance Mass VIII (*De Angelis*). The choir normally attended in the afternoon or evening for Vespers, to which might be attached Rosary or some other litany-style devotion, sermon, and Benediction of the Holy Sacrament. This evening service included hymns, both Latin and vernacular, fervently sung since they came from a smaller and more popular repertory than that of protestant churches.

Mass was not celebrated after mid-day, whereas nowadays, especially in Italy, evening masses oust other services and are frequently not choral. An enormous quantity of music composed for Mass, Vespers and Benediction fell into disuse even before the introduction of the vernacular liturgy— an amount far greater than was composed for protestant worship. It therefore includes both more of fine quality and more of poor quality. Unfortunately most continental cathedrals lack provision for music comparable with our choral foundations which maintain a daily, not just Sunday, repertory of choral music for the complete Kalendar. There may be colleges like Ouseley's foundation at Tenbury, sufficiently independent to maintain a historical repertory, but they would be bound by papal authority and would temper the ideals of founders to those expressed by the Vatican.

The Anglican Church is unique in being the creation of a Reformation settlement[1] that set up in place of the monastic prior and brotherhood a collegiate body, a permanent establishment of Dean and Chapter, boy choristers with their

---

[1] This is not written chauvinistically. This settlement poses problems and burdens anglican cathedrals with traditions which many churchmen wish to see modified or revoked.

school and masters, precentor, organist, and lay clerks or vicars choral. Fortunately the pattern was followed at Westminster Cathedral, but on the continent such a boys' choir and school survived the turmoils of Reformation and Counter-Reformation in very few cathedrals, papal or protestant. The "Vienna Boys' Choir" became moribund before its revival in this century, and it survived not because it was attached to St. Stephen's Cathedral but because it belonged to the Imperial Chapel with the famous school at which Schubert and other great musicians were educated. It has already been mentioned that Ratisbon (or Regensburg) was almost the only other continental cathedral which retained its boys' choir and school, notably revived in the nineteenth century. Ratisbon, not Rome, was the centre for editions of "golden age" liturgical music prepared by Haberl, Proske and others and also the place in which to hear its best performance. Some choirs and schools, such as the Lutheran one associated with Bach at Leipzig, lost their distinctive service as late as the eighteenth century, but it is safe to say that where we find an endowed boys' choir it is a comparatively modern revival suggested by the proximity of an orphanage or seminary or secured by the efforts of a patron or a music-loving cleric. Mixed choirs or small but efficient male choirs were and are the forces for which most Roman Catholic composers throughout the nineteenth century wrote their liturgical music. Italy favoured masses, motets and canticles in *three* vocal parts with organ; the soprano–alto did not often go higher than E, but the Italian tenors love a high tessitura. Right back in Rossini's day the three-voice choir was usual in Italy.

2. THE EIGHTEENTH CENTURY TRADITION

The tradition of church composition received by most Roman Catholics during the first decades of the nineteenth century was based on tastes set during the previous century by court chapels and by churches or aristocratic patronage. In German-speaking countries taste was formed notably by Vienna and the cathedrals or prince-bishops in Salzburg, Passau, Würzburg, Mainz, etc. Those which were only diocesan cathedrals and not court chapels could not always engage orchestral players, yet Schubert's masses for the Leichtenthal parish church and Spohr's and Rheinberger's for St. Peter's and St. Michael's in Munich show how parish churches in large cities might secure orchestras. We should not take the best known masses of Haydn, Mozart and Schubert as guides to the wider repertory, but we can notice what these men wrote when told to be brief, to avoid repeating words, to exclude long instrumental passages and brilliant accompaniments. (Mozart's complaints to Padre Martini show that they sometimes obeyed under protest.) Thus Mozart's mass in C (the "Trinity", K. 167, not the "Coronation") has simple organ accompaniment and a concentrated but frequently contrapuntal vocal style. Even his distinctive mannerisms are not easily recognisable when he must be brief and conservatively contrapuntal rather than his operatic self. He asks for soloists but cannot spread their melodies and decorative accompaniments to remind us of the pilaster volutes and figures in the rococo churches of his own day. In a *missa brevis* Mozart follows the Reutters, Fux, or even baroque composers like Caldara and Lotti: in a festal, commissioned mass he follows the most popular of his immediate predecessors, Hasse. If we must know from Mozart what was thought seemly by the church officials of his time we should examine his C minor mass for the consecration of Waisenhaus Church, K. 139, or the decidedly short and severe D minor mass, K. 65. Yet these, the least known and least personal of Mozart's masses, are mentioned only because the reader can examine them in collected editions, not because they best represent workday liturgical music, for how many churches could muster the singers and players for the least operatic of Mozart's masses? I have fortunately been able to examine at leisure and without expense a quantity of music sung by members of a seminary from about 1790 onwards.

3. EARLY NINETEENTH CENTURY

It will be remembered that in Tudor and Stuart times most of the Roman Catholic priests who braved the penal laws by coming to Great Britain were trained at the English College of Douai in the diocese of Arras. Nothing now remains of this famous building, which became a hospital soon after 1790. During the disturbances of revolutionary France its members left for various unobtrusively situated colleges in England where educated opinion was moving towards religious toleration. Sympathy for them was helped by horror at revolutionary atrocities, the treatment of the church in France and the steady arrival of other emigrants. Just at the turn of the century the priests of the northern counties (which included more catholic gentry than the southern and which received many Irish workers) sought the founding of a northern seminary, its senior members including men from Douai. Their desires were fulfilled by the founding of Ushaw College near Durham, where I have been shown much music used by Roman Catholics in France and England from the late eighteenth century to the present day—not what was used with orchestra and solosits but what was thought most worthy of preparation by men who would rehearse under whichever of their members could best guide them.

To this day Ushaw has no paid organist or choirmaster for its magnificent chapel, and it is interesting to note that most of its music directors, including the present one who is also Vice-President, have sought to perform what was officially approved. I have stayed in Italian seminaries and admit *some* attempt to follow the *motu proprio* but I cannot but be amused at their exiguous use of plainsong and their crude singing of it. It is even more difficult to reconcile official directives with what is heard at St. Peter's, especially on such occasions as the enthronement of a pope. This is not written in malice, for I thoroughly enjoy the feeling that worshippers are "being themselves", whether in a Welsh chapel, the abbey of Solesmes or an Italian church, and wish they were more often themselves in churches of my own communion. I have mentioned the difference between Ushaw and Italian seminaries merely because what is sung in places for the training of parish clergy (as distinct from what is done in Benedictine communities like Solesmes or Ampleforth, or in cathedrals) reflects what is sung in the parishes which the students will come to serve.

At Ex. 11 are specimens of music sung at Ushaw when the college first moved there. Though some of it must have been copied at Douai it is similar to music now in public archives but once used in the embassy chapels frequented by London catholics during the years of suppression.[1] The extracts at Ex. 11 are given in chronological order, as judged from the music paper and from such details as clefs, shapes of notes, change from quill to steel pens. We note the conservative dignity of the specimens first quoted; they belong to the age of Bach and Handel (or earlier) and come from volumes into which have also been copied masses, motets and canticles by Leo, Carissimi and Pitoni. The later examples reflect a change of style from strong baroque to late Georgian and early Victorian. Where names of composers are given they belong chiefly to Italians until we reach V. Novello, S. Wesley[2] and S. Webbe, three names we cannot suppose to have been well known outside Great Britain nor probably

[1] The only surviving embassy chapel in London is now the Church of Our Lady and St. Gregory in Warwick St., off Regent St. It was formerly the Chapel of the Bavarian Embassy, and owns a fine collection of music sung there in the early nineteenth century. There is also some at St. James's, Spanish Place, though this cathedral-like church was never the Spanish Embassy Chapel. The Spanish Embassy building is across the road (George St.) and now houses the Wallace Collection.

[2] S. Wesley's superb unaccompanied motets, *In exitu Israel*, *Omnia vanitas*, *Exsultate Deo*, and *Dixit Dominus* are rarely heard except as anglican cathedral anthems or during concerts by enterprising choral societies. (Some are obviously psalms for Vespers.) Their general neglect is a matter for reproach.

A.

Dixit Dominus [Leo?]

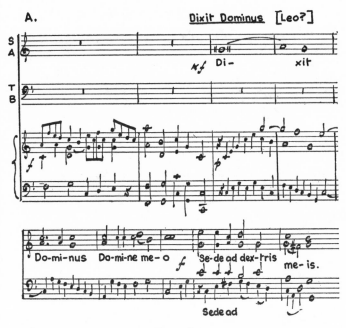

Ex. 11A

B.

O salutaris Hostia, Barsanti,

Ex. 11B

c.

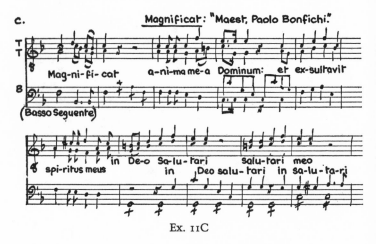

Ex. 11C

D.

Ex. 11D

Ex. 12

were some of the Italians, for few are worth an entry in reference books and those one recognises, like Barsanti,[1] were migrants.

Knowing that Vincent Novello was an enthusiastic Roman

[1] Francesco Barsanti, b. Lucca 1690, d. London about 1775. Violinist, flautist and composer, chiefly of concertos and overtures. For many years a prominent musician in Edinburgh, therefore well known in the north. Went to London in old age and played viola at Covent Garden and in Vauxhall Gardens, living with his daughter, a famous singer.

Catholic we need not wonder that his publishing business supplied liturgical music for his fellow churchmen as they approached the time (the 1830s) of political enfranchisement and the freedom to build churches and schools. Novello was in charge of music at the Portuguese Embassy Chapel and used Viennese masses. His own melodious and undisturbing style, a parallel with that of Attwood and Sterndale Bennett, fairly represents what was supplied by the organists and music directors of this country who were employed in chapels of embassies of catholic aristocrats. Perhaps the least sentimental and most reliable among them was Samuel Webbe (1740–1816) who, as organist to the Bavarian Embassy, was influenced by good, solid German music, though he was also organist to the Sardinian Chapel. Webbe's composition is often pedestrian but never vulgar. He published in 1794 a small book of *Masses for Small Choirs* and another of *Motetts or Antiphons*, and from some of the latter we have taken worthy tunes for our hymn books, e.g. that to "Come thou holy Paraclete" (*E. H. 155*).

Very little of this British music is found in the Ushaw books except in manuscript. When the English seminaries began to buy printed music they favoured neither British nor Italian; the bulk of their repertory was by German-speaking composers, and for this they were very much to be commended. Setting after setting by German catholic composers makes most anglican nineteenth century music seem amateurish; but let us note the state of music nearer the seat of papal authority and so justify the preference for German settings.

4. OPERATIC MID-CENTURY MUSIC

The famous *motu proprio* of 1903 was but the final formulation of a whole century of attempts to establish a seemly church style, but reformers had to deal with Italian love of operatic expression and instrumental *concertato*. Even if the latter were merely represented by an organ the admired organist was he who best evoked the variety and colour of the theatre band. The triumph of the cathedral *cappella musicale* or of the parochial *coro* was a tremendous blast of voices and instruments interlarded with *arie* and *ariette* (i.e. large and small operatic solos) to mark a feast, a really solemn day! To secure the admired musical structures, from fugues to cavatinas, words might be repeated, sentences and paragraphs dissected and dramatic pauses introduced. Many choir directors made a practice of fitting the sacred texts to opera melodies. Perhaps the *ne plus ultra*, from portions of Rossini's operas, came from the hand of one Melchorre Balbi who in 1869 patched up a Requiem Mass in honour of that composer. Rome's most famous opera singers were impressed into the performance, which drew forth such applause (led by the officiating cardinal!) that the music had to be repeated as a sacred concert.[1] One Alessandro Capuana, unable to set a complete mass by ransacking Rossini's brisk and jumpy rhythms, Bellini's elegiac airs and Donizetti's hilarious tunes, was driven to *Don Giovanni* for his *Credo*! (Ex. 12). Even long after the *motu proprio* popular Italian church composers wrote organ parts like the accompaniments of operas, with many arpeggio figures and little connective tunes with dotted quavers and pizzicato bass effects. I do not say this with disapproval, for I am no lover of the "harmonium" legato with never a rest—as old examination papers used to say, "Always in four *flowing* parts". The organ accompaniments of most English nineteenth century composers add little life to their compositions.

5. THE CECILIAN REFORMERS

We should not suppose that the Roman hierarchy waited until late in the nineteenth century before setting forth its

[1] Most of the information given here about Italian church music was obtained from Mgr. Ernesto Moneta Caglio, principal of the Milan Pontifical Institute of Sacred Music, who will shortly issue a comprehensive history of catholic church music during the nineteenth century.

ideals of *distinctive* church music.[1] Alexander VII in 1657, Innocent XII in 1692 and Benedict XIV (Constitution *Annus qui*, 1749) had spoken pertinently against frivolity and worldly ostentation in liturgical music; among later popes who reminded musicians of regulations promulgated by their predecessors were Leo XII in 1824 and Pius VIII in the brief "Bonum est confiteri Domino" of 1830. The influence of the south German restorers and of "Cecilian" scholars is seen in the *Coeremoniale episcoporum* of 1886 and the *Regolamento* of the Sacred Congregation of Rites of 1894, but the immediate predecessor of the famous *motu proprio*, indeed almost its first draft, is a pastoral letter by Cardinal Giuseppe Sarto, Patriarch of Venice, who later promulgated the *motu proprio* as Pope Pius X. Other diocesan instructions echoed his. The *motu proprio* normally stopped orchestral masses except in Bavaria; it sensibly did not issue an index of forbidden music. Its promoters seemed most concerned to reduce the length of settings and the inept repetition of words.

Though the *motu proprio* comes three years beyond this survey, one should record the fact that it influenced most Christian churches, and that they have been glad to quote its admirable phrases in support of their own efforts towards reforms. Almost the only questionable sentences in it were justified at the time. There is always this difficulty with recommendations which remain in force until revoked by another pontiff. An example of this is the forbidding of priests to enter opera houses or theatres without special permission, though they may go freely to other public entertainments, such as cinemas or circuses; when the rule was made, opera theatres were the favourite venue of gallants bent upon disreputable enamouring. In the *motu proprio* there is a clause forbidding the piano in church. This exclusion was justified in 1903 when the piano must immediately have

[1] I have, I hope, already made it clear that I question the precise wishes of reformers in all denominations while commending their care for church music.

reminded congregations of some other occupation than worship; it was associated with the dance, the eating house, the musical party at home, and the concert, whereas the organ had not yet invaded the theatre—nor the cinema-theatre which had yet to come. Over sixty years later, when the clean sound of a good piano would be more pleasant than that of the nasty old organs which most small parishes cannot afford to rebuild, and when the piano is no longer specially associated with secular occupations, Roman Catholic churches which cannot afford organs use the vilest of all accompanimental instruments—the harmonium. Unfortunately so do many small protestant churches, but in Italy one can attend service in a cathedral with a splendid organ and famous organist who accompanies the choir for the items of the Ordinary while, in extreme contrast, the items of the Proper are sung by clerics and servers to the accompaniment of a chancel harmonium. Accompanied plainchant is in any case a worse artistic outrage than anglican chanting; the addition of a harmonium makes it more damnable.

The *motu proprio* should not be blamed for unattainable ideals. Many priests and music directors who wish to carry out its recommendations cannot do so with their congregations, or could not until the liturgical movement became generally understood. Until recently most folk were quite unused to modal music: modal flavours are now ubiquitous in "pop", which lags in harmonic and melodic styles behind "highbrow" advances. Moreover schoolchildren since the 1920s have become more and more familiar with folk song and dance. Until well on in our own century "Gregorians" sounded like dirges, harmonised in minor keys even when the melody was modal.

When I first heard music by Palestrina (*The Aeterna Christi Munera* mass at a Choral Eucharist in St. Paul's) I thought it dull, with far too many full closes in the same two keys. I do not think I was mistaken. I heard what was done and not what I was told to hear. Music by Victoria and Palestrina was then held to be "mystical" (the word was not defined) and super-refined, and it was thought correct to sing it very slowly and "floatingly", with no suggestion of vigour or passion, no moulding of phrases, no attempt even in *Credo* or *Gloria* to let the words "come trippingly off the tongue". There were not the informed clergy and musicians to teach in all parishes what the Roman hierarchy desired. Radio and the gramophone have probably done more than other teaching for plainsong and polyphony. They cannot be learnt and loved just by lectures. They are sung best in colleges and communities whose members are not picked for their musical ability but for their religious vocation; daily, not just weekly, they sing offices to no other music, and ideally they have no instrument to support them. The freshmen's timid mumblings or mistakes are carried by the unison of his seniors; after less than six months he knows by heart the psalter and most of the masses; after six years he knows the propers. It is precisely when the *words* are thus known that the chant, firmly associated with them, becomes the most perfect vehicle for praying them. Curiously enough, it also comes to be the most easy and "natural" one. Is anything like this possible with congregations that gather only on Sundays? For that matter is it possible with their choirs?

I shall not attempt to answer the question except to say that in certain French and German cathedrals where the main Sunday service is at 9.00 a.m. or 9.30 a.m. ("Low Mass with extras, including music") and where one plainchant setting, usually Mass VIII or Mass XVI, is used invariably, I have heard large congregations participating heartily in the music and evidently enjoying it. The experience has seemed so exactly what church music should be that I have forgotten to curse the organ accompaniment! On two occasions I wondered why I found myself boldly joining in though I was not certain of the words. It was because both the officiant and his two acolytes (in lay dress) at the altar, as well as a director of vernacular devotions in the pulpit, knew how to use micro-phones well. The worshipper seemed to be enveloped yet not overwhelmed with voices, as if his neighbours in the crowd held the melody and words securely and he was as happy as the freshman seminarist I have just mentioned.

6. GERMAN INFLUENCE

I do not wish to minimise the work of scholar-reformers, but it rarely appeals to people with little musical or general culture. Readers of James Joyce may recall how Bloom and Dedalus mused on the "beautiful old masses of Rossini". For most congregations until past 1900 a "solemn" mass or a "beautiful" *Magnificat* or *O salutaris* was one with "arie, cavatine, duetti, terzetti finali" . . . and, of course, stromenti (encyclical *Bonum est confiteri Domino* of Leo X in 1830, chiefly directed against division of sacred words as if for characters in operas), and they were not disposed to exchange these delights for plainsong and Palestrina.

We have noted that the restoration-reform movement began in Germany. Right back in the eighteenth century German clerics and musicians were objecting to secularity. Johann Bähr, music director at the court of Weissenfels, in his *Musical Discourse* of 1719, inveighs against "merry fugues" to penitential words yet does not object to "splendidly performed" court masses, because "the communicant may be full of devotion though he be grandly dressed". Meinrad Spiess, in charge of music at the monastery of Irsee near Munich, complained in his book on composition (1746) that "young musicians tamely follow their elders when they set words which mean 'Lord have mercy' to rhythms suitable for a dance". I need not bore the reader by continuing the list. German-speaking Catholics, both during the nineteenth century and before it, felt a guilt which their co-religionists in Latin countries did not as they enjoyed in church what reminded them of the theatre. Moreover during the seventeenth and eighteenth centuries fine organ playing and organ building affected catholic Germany as did emulation of Lutheran singing. When Handel came to London he practised upon the organ at St. Paul's because that was the only one he could find with pedals. The contribution of the organ to public worship in England was so purely ornamental that in the average parish church it was no more essential than bell ringing. In Germany the preludes, fugues and toccatas served that purpose, but the treatments of chorales and much of the extemporising was liturgical—within the service, commenting upon the words and action or connecting them. It was listened to as a devotion. Futhermore it must not be supposed, just because Bach and other Lutherans were the greatest exponents of this art, that it was confined to protestant churches.

It had for some time puzzled me that fine organ pieces on chorales came (after Bach's time) from catholic organists—indeed that most of the German organ composers of the nineteenth century from Rheinberger to Reger were Catholics and that they, more than others, derived their art from Bach. Then soon after the war I was stationed on an airfield at Wahn, a village near Cologne, where I attended morning service. My first surprise was the quality of the organ playing. The instrument was a two-manual American organ with pedals, and though I detest imitations of proper organs this one was capable of playing a trio-sonata. The schoolmistress-organist would have shamed many a city player in this country, not because she was more clever but because she was more careful, and made all she did a contribution to the particular service—a sung mass with very little ceremonial. Her extemporisation was exemplary in its modesty and discretion; it was thematic yet fashioned in clearly cadenced periods that allowed her to finish at any point without smudge or fluster. This was not the formless churning we hear even on state occasions in England.

My next surprise was the big congregation beginning service with *Lobe den Herren*. Four chorales which I had thought were exclusively Lutheran punctuated that Mass; the *Credo* was to plainchant (No. 1) but the rest of the ordinary was choral in four parts, sung by the mixed forces in the "organ" gallery, chiefly schoolboys and schoolgirls but several adults also. They sounded German-solid and I turned round to see Fräulein very firmly conducting. The music was pedestrian but far better, less trivial, more thematic than the average used in my choirboy days. Afterwards I went up into the gallery and found that this was a Mass by Ett, whom we mentioned above as one of the Ratisbon restorers. My third surprise was to hear so much of the mass in German —not by the priest, who stayed at the altar with his two acolytes, but by a man in a frock coat who stood near the entrance to the chancel and pronounced the prayers in a loud voice while the priest whispered them in Latin. I was told that he was called the *Vorsprecher*. The only German I heard from the priest was a repetition of the Gospel and his ensuing sermon and notices.

This experience led me to other villages in Rhineland and, of course, to town churches. In some the service was High Mass, yet in most of them one met vernacular speaking and congregational chorales. The music was not always by German composers but included masses by Ravanello, Perosi and Refice, therefore in three parts; in some churches it was Haberl's or Proske's editions of Palestrina, Lassus, the Anerio brothers, Casciolini, etc., but in every church I heard the splendid singing of chorales, and good organ playing. I apologise to readers who are surprised at my surprise, but my previous knowledge of continental catholic services was confined to those of France before the war, most of which I thought execrable. I am bound also to say that Lutheran services (which I naturally associated with Schweitzer) were disappointing. In Rhineland and Switzerland the Protestants used few chorales of the Luther period and dragged their singing, though they also seemed to expect good organ playing.[1] A Jesuit enlightened me concerning the catholic en-

[1] I have to admit that I have not heard Lutheran worship in the Lutheran north of Germany. It was disappointing in protestant Stuttgart (Württemberg)

joyment of the Lutheran musical treasury. He said there was no single official hymn-book in catholic Germany and no general directive about the use of the vernacular; at that time the priest had to say the Latin mass. What I had witnessed, however, was a permissive diocesan usage which began back in the seventeenth century when German Catholics were attracted by the Lutheran chorales and vernacular prayers. Two years ago, as I alighted from the train to see the great cathedral at Speier, I heard many voices singing *Ein feste Burg* in the open air. Was not Speier in an overwhelmingly catholic area? I took a taxi in the direction of the music. The crowds were assembled for a Eucharistic Congress and were singing *Ein feste Burg* during an open air High Mass, Luther's ghost no doubt approving.

These experiences have led me to suppose that the Ushaw books reflect reliably what was sung in churches aligned with the Cecilians (rather colourless as original composers) but ready to enjoy more merry fare on feast days. Much of their printed repertory seems to have been by Bavarian, Rhenish, Franconian or Dutch provenance. A pencilled note suggests that on All Souls Day, 1888, Ushaw sang Casciolini's Requiem for three-part men's voices, and on the following Sunday a mass by Jacob Blied. I know little about him except that this piece was in a volume of masses printed "Ratisbonae, Neo Eboraci et Cincinnati", so I presume its contents were widely used. Blied was evidently a Ratisbon "Nazarene", anticipating what arrived in anglican churches with Charles Wood's masses. Who can tell Blied from Casciolini in Ex. 13? On St. Andrew's Day that year Ushaw sang a mass by Ignaz Mitterer for "equal voices of two parts with organ", of which a specimen is given at Ex. 14. How much better is this pedestrian German music than contemporary pedestrian music of other countries!

---

but excellent in catholic Bavaria, notably so at fine modern *Mattauskirche* in Munich, surely a particularly cultured congregation, for one was aware of much "restoration".

7. POPULAR SETTINGS

One volume of "motets" at Ushaw is somewhat amusing in these oecumenically minded times. Most readers have surely seen old copies of classical masses supplied with English words (not translations, or the Prayer Book versions but such nonsense as *Kyrie eleison* paralleled with "List to my devotion"!)

Ex. 13

Ex. 14

in order that Victorian protestant tongues might not be sullied by the speech of the Scarlet Woman, though they would carouse in her musical delights. This volume entitled "*Cantica Sion*, or English Anthems set to Latin Words for the service of the Catholic Church, by a Priest of the Society of Jesus" could be exonerated from similar small mindedness but for its comic introduction. Since Latin was then required at Mass and Vespers, how grateful should Roman Catholics have been to this Rector of Stonyhurst in 1875 for making available Croft's "First Choral Mass" (!), Travers's *Te Deum*, Rogers's *Magnificat*, Purcell's *Rejoice*, Wise's *Prepare ye the way*, Blow's *The Lord hear thee*, Boyce's *By the waters of Babylon*, and even pieces by S. S. Wesley, Ouseley and Stainer! But the preface is an apology unconsciously commenting upon the bigotry of its age:

> My object is not to glorify protestant music, for these noble anthems are assuredly not Protestant but Catholic both in origin and inspiration. . . . With the Anglican Liturgy they have but the slightest possible connections. . . . Why should not catholic musicians be enabled to compete on an equal footing with their protestant fellow-countrymen?

Much else in this preface is hardly amusing, for it might have been written by the very type of Anglican of whose provincial tastes one despairs.

> Well would it be for us if, instead of wearing ourselves out in the never-ending dispute as to the merits of Mozart and Haydn [Who ever wore himself out in a dispute of which I have heard nothing?] we should devote our attention to the encouragement and cultivation of our own national music. There are men of real genius among us. [Our author wisely names none!] How long shall they lack incitement to produce, because we are in love with foreign wares which it is at least a question if the Church has not concurred?

A deliciously vague final animadversion! The extraordinary thing about this preface is that it sounds like the work of a narrow Anglican, not a travelled Jesuit whose name was De Vico. It is precisely the enforced experience of an international repertory, albeit containing nothing great, that gives the Roman Catholic musician an advantage over the Protestant. Unless he constantly refreshes his mind with opera, chamber music, etc., the anglican cathedral organist deteriorates quickly with his insular round. With what pleasure I heard Schubert being warbled when I last walked up the drive of the Royal School of Church Music!

But even obedient seminaries did not confine their attentions to German Cecilian and restored music. I should have loved to have heard Ushaw sing, as they often did if I may judge by the tattered copies, some of the three-part masses of Saviero Mercadante (1795–1870) which I have found in many a church cupboard. They, too, are nostalgically mentioned in Joyce's *Ulysses*. Mercadante richly deserved his popularity because of his professional competence. He was a poor Naples orphan who trained under Zingarelli and composed many operas, influencing Verdi; he shows, however, no trace of the "Nazarene" emulations of the German restorers. Nothing like Ex. 15 would have been issued with a mitral stamp from Ratisbon. Yet Mercadante has some personality as a musician and offers what voices and organist find worth the labour of rehearsal. Unfortunately one cannot rate so highly the church music of Ravanello and Perosi, composers whom Italian priests mention as soon as one says "We see little attempt to meet the demands of the hierarchy near the seat of authority!" Lorenzo Perosi (1872–1952) the son of a cathedral *maestro di cappella*, was a much more competent musician than most English church composers of his time except Stanford. Though intended for the priesthood from youth, he studied at the Milan Conservatory and wrote a number of dramatic oratorios on biblical subjects, some of which could be mounted on a stage and show considerable technical mastery, especially of the orchestra. Perosi then studied with Haberl at Regensberg, though it is hard to see what effect this had on his music. (I had a devout Italian among my students. I frequently commended his melodic and rhythmic vigour, the sheer delight in sound which he brought to academic exercise. I still cannot explain how it was possible for him to imitate plainsong and Palestrina without discernible solecism and yet make the result remind one of *Madam Butterfly*! (I envied him!)

The trouble with Perosi who, first at St. Mark's, Venice and then at the Sistine Chapel, was deservedly *persona grata* with

Ex. 15

the reforming pope, is that he achieved neither an imitative style like the Germans, nor a recognisably national one. His studies brought a conflict of ideals, pruned his luxuriance, but produced no highly characteristic style. The same could be said of Perosi's contemporary Oreste Ravanello, whose well-composed masses are as deservedly popular in Italy as Stanford's settings of the anglican ritual are in this country. Indeed the observation made about Perosi's music seems true of most good Italian church music—for instance the masses of Refice, one of Perosi's successors; yet it will be a great pity if modern movements, including the enforced setting of the mass to a vernacular text that lacks beauty or cadence, push into oblivion a repertory of better music than most. Perosi and his contemporaries showed an Italian delight in singing, in sound, in medium, allied to a competence in long-range composing that is rare among church musicians of this country. They could have written tolerable symphonies; most of us could not.

8. FRENCH CHURCH MUSIC

Berlioz's teacher, Lesueur,[1] reintroduced the orchestra into Notre Dame for Napoleon's coronation. During most of the nineteenth century it was used at fashionable Paris churches like the Madeleine and, certainly on great festivals, in the main churches or cathedrals or provincial cities, where among popular masses were those of Gounod, Ambroise Thomas, Guilmant, Tinel, Neukomm and Dubois. I cannot but suppose that histories of music mislead us into supposing that great influence was exerted *actually in the choice of church music* by the Schola Cantorum, founded by disciples of the famous Belgian who settled in Paris, César Franck, 1822–1890. These men were by no means exact counterparts of the Ratisbon scholars whose publications they welcomed and used, for it was not medieval and renaissance music that originally brought them together. Franck was no great researcher, but he had acquainted himself at the keyboard with a great deal of printed music and was well soaked in Bach as well as in Liszt and Wagner. His Walloon birth symbolises the mixture of French and German ideals in his music. He brought into the most racial and conservative of capitals

[1] Five of his inflated "oratorio" masses are in the Hirsch Library at the British Museum.

what was thought to be mystical and highly emotional German music, because of his rejection of classical conventions in works labelled "sonata", "quartet", symphony and so on, his obsessive modulations and turgidity. His personality, thought modest and gentle, elicited near-adoration from the young.

D'Indy's *César Franck* for many years gave us a false picture of "Pater seraphicus", for Franck's churchmanship was solid and sensible. His saintly appearance hid a strong constitution, and he had qualities which gave him a happy domestic life with a beautiful and spirited wife who had been an actress, whereas poor Berlioz reaped misery from his adored lady Franck's orthodox catholicism did not incur the ecstasies and torments of certain types of mystic, nor was it demonstrative, yet it became a matter for admiration and envy among those already disposed to admire the man who opened their minds to tracts of music and artistic expression which the formal courses of the Conservatoire did not.

There is little in Franck's own church music that would be thought exemplary by the Haberl group or the later Cecilians. The popular "Panis angelicus" fairly represents the rest. His best masses are the one for bass solo with organ and the Op. 12 *Messe à 3 voix*; and one could paraphrase one of his songs (for instance "La Procession") and feel no great discrepancy. Franck is best classed with his admired and admiring Liszt as a church composer. Like Liszt he was romantically fascinated by plainchant intonations and even published a volume of accompaniments and "vocal arrangements" of "Gregorian Services" (*cultes grégoriennes*) which, one hopes, are by now used only documentarily. Perhaps his greatest achievement lay, like Liszt's, in advancing the forms of music. One itches to clean and rewrite some of Liszt's symphonic poems. If one can resist a similar mental impudence one can enjoy Franck's organ works, especially the *Trois Chorals*, as some of the most interesting compositions of the whole century.

Franck's value to church musicians lay less in his church music than in their identification of an avant-garde artist with firm churchmanship. The organ class conceded to him by the Conservatoire became a school within a school, teaching a good deal more than organ music. The most significant part of that "good deal more" lay in its attitude to instruction in composition. This we deduce from D'Indy's *Cours de Composition* which is not a manual applying "How to do it" to various structures and tasks facing the composer in this or that kind of opera, orchestral piece, sonata, etc. but a selective guide to acknowledged masterpieces of composition. If D'Indy reflects his master's methods then Franck had the sense to know that, by definition, original composition is unteachable. "Our object" writes D'Indy, "is to provide favourable conditions for genius . . . by critical study of musical masterpieces." When Franck died his disciples sought to continue his famous class as an institution in its own right; they formed the Schola Cantorum with D'Indy as Director of Studies, Charles Bordes, Guilmant and others as teachers. Though its original purpose was restoration (plainchant and polyphony) and the improvement of church music,[1] it remained until well after 1900 associated with an avant-garde, thereafter gradually acquiring a reputation for pedantic orthodoxy. It had enormous influence upon the general culture of musicians, including church musicians, because it had branches at Marseilles, Lyons, Bordeaux and many other big French cities, as well as in South America. In the capital its regular concerts were invaluable, for they included newly discovered works by Monteverdi, Lully, Rameau, Gluck, Haydn, etc., as well as recitals of folk music and pieces by modern composers. Thus the Schola Cantorum was not, despite its original aim, a French Ratisbon. It was, so to speak, "on the side of the angels" as regards the ideals of the *motu proprio* because (*a*) one of its founders, Bordes, familiarised members with polyphonic masters through the choir he called *Les Chanteurs de Saint Gervais*, still flourishing. It sang

[1] Its premises in the Rue Saint-Jacques once belonged to the English Benedictines and were the burial place of James II's remains.

first from the new German editions but came to publish its own. (*b*) Pupils of the Schola were familiarised with the publications and commentaries of the Solesmes monks.

Yet the Schola Cantorum was not founded until 1894 and the fruits of its work were reaped chiefly in our present century. It is probable that one man's early death prevented France from being ahead of European "restoration" in all liturgical music and not just in plainchant. Alexandre Étienne Choron (1771–1834) was a scientific and historical scholar, armed with several languages, before he turned to musicology. He used his limited fortune in publishing both music and treatises on music originally issued between about 1600 and 1800, and he also produced a three-volume *Principles of Composition;* but he was unfortunately associated with the restored Bourbon monarchy, and when the 1830 revolution dethroned Louis XVIII, Choron lost state support for the *Institution Royale de Musique Classique et Religieuse* of which he was founder and director. As far as I know his neo-polyphonic unaccompanied mass, for three voices, and his *Méthode de plain-chant* of 1825 antedate any comparable undertakings.

In 1853 Louis Niedermeyer, a Swiss musician who, despite his friendship with and patronage by Rossini, was consistently unsuccessful as an opera composer, set up in Paris his *École de Musique Réligieuse et Classique* which soon became simply the *École Niedermeyer*. The choice of its original title was plainly a tribute to Choron, and certainly its primary purpose was the training of organists and church choirmasters; indeed it has since enrolled some very distinguished students— Fauré was for ten years its alumnus—but its most valuable work, like that of the Schola Cantorum, has been among the mass of local musicians and fine teachers of sterling worth who do not achieve international distinction but are the backbone of musical life in church and nation. Niedermeyer was no Choron or Haberl yet his many masses and other church pieces were, for their period, refined, attractive and well composed.

It is most likely that in provincial cities and villages, where a Niedermeyer or Schola Cantorum musician or cleric had influence, better church music was to be heard during the last decades of the nineteenth century than was heard in many a society church in Paris. What we lack in this more seemly music for churches of limited resources is the variety of styles and designs in the setting of liturgical texts by the greater composers from Gounod to Bruckner. Unable myself to say from such information as I have collected which composers' works were most widely bought by continental catholic churches during the second half of the nineteenth century, I sought the opinion of Mr. Michael Dawney, Scholar of Lincoln College, Oxford, who turned over hundreds of nineteenth century masses while preparing a thesis for the degree of B.Litt. He is unwilling to suggest any order of popularity, but the following list of names seems to bear out the impression I drew from the Ushaw books—that these composers were not just beloved nationally. Neukomm, for instance, who published no less than fifty masses, shows his Austrian origin in his music; yet he was popular in Italy, Rhineland, England, France (he died in Paris 1858), Spain and Portugal, where he was at one time the Lisbon director of church music. These were the prolific church composers whose masses are to be found in the British Museum collections: Raffaele Carcano, Emile Dethier, Paul Fauchey, Benoit Constant Fauconier, Robert Fuhrer, Johannes Habert, Saviero Mercadante, Ignaz Mitterer, Sigismund von Neukomm, Pietro Parmeggiani, Luigi Felice Rossi, Cesare de Sanctis, Theodor Zimmers; the popular German composers have been already named; the popular French ones were Guilmant, Tinel, Gigout and Dubois. The popular composers known only in Austria and south Germany are too numerous to recount without presuming that those mentioned were more in demand than other. This chapter is already rather long, but surely more important to the English reader than those on music with which he is all too familiar.

5

English Choir Music

1. CATHEDRAL MUSIC IN DECLINE AND REVIVAL

Because this book is written in England it must give disproportionate space to music of the established church of Great Britain and Ireland, hereinafter called for convenience "The Anglican Church" with apologies to Irish, Scottish and Welsh episcopalians who have secured a measure of freedom. Between Boyce and Greene in the eighteenth century and Stanford, whose first works became known just before the opening of the twentieth century, no composer produced any music for anglican choirs or organs that is deemed worth mention in a general history of music. This does not mean that they failed to serve their Church, but that, since none of them was a composer of even second rank, none now serves us as he served his contemporaries.

The exception might have been Samuel Wesley, 1766–1837, if he had not joined the Roman Church in 1784. One marvels that thousands did not either follow him or else join protestant dissenters during an era of anglican torpor and disgrace. It was after 1784 and increasingly after the accident to his skull in 1787 that Samuel Wesley wrote his finest music[1] and pursued his study of J. S. Bach. In 1810 he began editorial work which led to the issue of Bach's trio-sonatas, the *Well Tempered Keyboard* and the English version of Forkel's

[1] He fell into a builder's excavation on a dark night. The thought of surgery before the coming of anaesthetics is horrifying and he cannot be blamed for declining to be trepanned without assurance of success. At first he suffered only periods of derangement and disablement, but undoubtedly his mishap deprived us of many fine works, secular as well as sacred.

Life of Bach. Samuel Wesley was in his day a better composer than his son who, like so many other English musicians of the nineteenth century, wrote no other music than pieces for choir and organ. Samuel wrote symphonies,[1] concertos for piano and for organ with orchestra (which the B.B.C. seems to be exploring), a great amount of music for piano, string quartets and a quintet. Much of his music awaits modern editions, but church musicians may be blamed for failing to use what is available in printed and inexpensive copies. Occasionally we hear a lifeless "anthem" performance of *Exsultate Deo*, or its translation *Sing aloud with gladness*. There was a time when some college chapels used the magnificent eight-part *In exitu Israel;* but for every fifty cathedral services which broadcast some feeble work by Sebastian Wesley do we once hear such pieces by his father as that quoted at Ex. 16, which shows the beginning and the ending of the work? In his secular instrumental works Samuel Wesley belongs to the age of Hummel and Weber, but conservative dignity, fortified by his love of Bach, makes his church music point more to the eighteenth than to the romantic century; it rarely melts to his son's or Attwood's lyricism, yet it is always better than theirs in the total piece, and better than any English church music until the arrival of Stanford, the next British composer capable of writing long instrumental movements.

If our duty were only to examine music for its enduring worth, not even the considerable merits of *sections* in the church music (the only music) of Samuel Sebastian Wesley, 1810–1876, would make this more than a short chapter. The reasons for this are not contained in the sociological and psychological diagnoses so beloved by modern critics when they are disappointed, but in the plain fact that Nature did not produce native composers of outstanding genius, secular or sacred. Had she done so, this country would have been undeservedly favoured. If we write down the names of European states and

[1] One of which in B flat is a magnificent work influenced by Haydn's London symphonies.

their approximate populations in 1600, 1650, 1700, 1750 and so on, and add the names of the nine first-rate and sixteen second-rate musical geniuses that have lived since 1600, we first marvel that one city, Vienna, held for many years the

Ex. 16

"great Four", almost half of the first-raters, and then we note that our own small island bred at least two first-raters and four second-raters. Why grumble that she bred none of either rank between Purcell and Elgar? Why suppose that political or social conditions can turn talent into genius? Where are the great composers of lucky Switzerland? Copland is the

D

nearest America has produced to a first-rate genius, and can anyone reproach America for failing to lavish opportunity on talent? What great favours did Bach enjoy in Leipzig? Genius is not utterly suppressed by adversity, nor even by its possessor's faults. Berlioz's huge undertakings show glaring faults, but they do not prevent recognition of his unique genius, or of his imagination.

It is true, nevertheless, that adverse conditions, such as the widespread Philistinism of early Victorian England (including her reforming public schools) can prevent genius or talent from producing as much of its best expression as it might. Thus was allowed to run shallow the talent that might have served a virile church in the man who was organist of St. Paul's when the century opened. He was Thomas Attwood 1765–1838, a musician whom Englishmen hold in esteem because, after studying in Naples, he went to lodge with and be taught by Mozart in Vienna, and Mozart declared him to be one of his favourite pupils. Attwood had no need to lean upon sacred words. He wrote many piano sonatas and songs as well as preludes and fugues for the organ; but he was best known in London for nearly forty ballad operas or plays with music given at various theatres between about 1790 and 1830. At its level his familiar setting of "Come, Holy Ghost, our souls inspire" is nothing short of perfect—an epithet one cannot apply to most works of greater men; but oh the pity that this tender but clean Mozartian lyricism was not engaged on other church pieces! Attwood's settings range from the pleasant to the insipid, yet as if to prove that his best might have been drawn from him more often if it had been demanded, we meet among the anthems collected by his godson, Walmisley, a splendid *I was glad*, commissioned for the coronation of George IV.

Because of the moribund state of the Anglican Church from the beginning of the century to almost its middle (reforms were not immediately manifest in the cathedrals and choral foundations) many talented church composers survive by just one or two pieces. "National Apostasy" was the theme of Newman's famous assize sermon at Oxford, regarded as launching the Tractarian or Oxford Movement although its followers in Cambridge were more concerned with the arts and worship. Methodism had been a recall by high Anglicans to the catholic practices of prayer, fasting, almsgiving, penitence, meditation upon the scriptures, the kind of experience now called a retreat, and the frequent and devout reception of Holy Communion.[1] If Methodism had been embraced by the established church as it was by many parish incumbents not only would another schism have been avoided but also timely changes in the mind and worship of churchmen would have occurred before they were accompanied by controversy and "party" forming. During Queen Victoria's reign and in comfortable areas even Methodism lost its missionary vitality and became as smug as the established church—pew rents and all—yet it was the dissenters who cared for the unschooled industrial poor before the state church produced devoted slum priests, Lowthers, Stantons, Dollings and Dykeses, settlements of religious communities and overworked sisterhoods in cities, training colleges and schools for the fortunate and for the less fortunate who "rose" with education.

The retailing of a few facts will spare lengthy discussion of the state of cathedral music in Barchester's heyday. S. S. Wesley wrote *The Wilderness* at the request of the Dean of Hereford for performance on Easter Day 1833, the year of

---

[1] Wesley's diary tells of 3,000 and 4,000 communicants at a time during the brothers' missions in Leeds and Halifax parish churches, and of the necessity to compose eucharistic hymns for use during the long administration "to keep alive the fervour of those waiting as harangues could not". (How much our would-be liturgiologists today, with their services stuffed with oblique harangues in the guise of prayers and praises, have to learn from the eighteenth century!) Let anyone who doubts the churchmanship of the Wesleys read Charles's hymn *Victim Divine*, especially the lines at the close—"To ev'ry faithful soul appear, And shew thy real Presence here". I have often wondered why the "high" editors of *A. and M.* and *E. H.* omitted two verses of this hymn which prolong the imagery of sacrifice and incense!

Newman's sermon. The deputy system worked so badly that there were no men in the choir except a bass who was tied to duty because he happened to be the Dean's butler. By running from one service to another as soon as the anthem was over the men of St. Paul's and Westminster (or their deputies) managed also to form the paid choirs of two chapels royal. C. A. Belli, Precentor of St. Paul's during the first fifty years of Victoria's reign, so infrequently entered his cathedral that when he attempted to do so for Wellington's funeral he was refused admittance. His stipend exceeded the sum of payments to the whole choir. In 1815 St. Paul's had only eight boys, who were neither boarded nor properly educated. They received £5 per annum. The lay clerks received £60 and could be given notice of dismissal without pension when they grew old. The boys left when their voices broke. It was possible for a cleric to hold the office of precentor at three cathedrals simultaneously. From their cathedral appointments and their parishes major canons received emolument which normally totalled at least £1,000—more than £5,500 by today's value—and this incurred only three months' cathedral duty in the year. They could avoid it by sending a deputy. A dean might hold the bishopric of a diocese at the other end of the country from his cathedral.

The writings of S. S. Wesley while organist at Hereford (1832), Exeter (1835), Leeds Parish Church (of which more later), Winchester (1849) and Gloucester (1865) are amply quoted in several books. Suffice it here to quote only something he wrote just after he went to Winchester: "If he (an able and keen organist) gives trouble in his attempts at improvement he will be, by some chapters, at once voted a person with whom they 'cannot get on smoothly' and 'a bore'." The heroine of anglican musicians is Miss Maria Hackett, a wealthy lady called "The Choristers' Friend" because between 1810 and 1835 she paid regular visits to all cathedrals in the country, pleaded with their clergy for reforms, protested against the treatment of singers and organists, disbursed sums for needy boys and arranged for the welfare and education of others. Her campaign began at St. Paul's where, according to recollections of Sir John Goss when he had become the organist, the boys had "only minimal instruction in the Three Rs on three days of the week".

The most considerable anglican musician who saw the dawn of reform has the credit for being its advocate. As we shall see when we deal with parish churches he was associated with a notable clerical reformer. Samuel Sebastian Wesley was by manner and temperament a "character", yet during his last forty years his opinion was sought upon appointments of musicians and upon music itself. No English organist was more respected, and in consequence what was admired in him may have become the fault of future generations. We need caution in saying so, for our salutary reactions against much in Victorian music may prejudice our esteem of its noblest promoters. His contemporaries wrote of Wesley as a "great" organist. To hear him was to be ashamed of one's own playing and to make resolutions. He was particularly admired for his extemporisations "after the psalms" and "before the sermon". He had so large a hand that he could stretch one and a half octaves of the keyboard and he demanded from his pupils mastery of a *legato* that disguised the resistance of tracker action. The touch of English organs was made heavy by couplers and the addition of stops. Today our ideal is of crisp phrasing, and we no longer associate *legato* with *religioso* except in mockery.

We wonder if we should now think Wesley a "great" organist fit to compare with Germans and Frenchmen. Was his extemporisation admirable or did it promote the chord-churning without rhythmic interest and motive development, without a planned bass, without relief of combined manual-pedal stodge, that disgraces our cathedrals on national and public occasions when the titular organist directs and the assistant strums? A village church and instrument would reveal this pretentious rubbish for what it is. There is no excuse for it, for coronations, state weddings and funerals, special commemorations, etc., are rehearsed and timed for broadcasting. Organists know when and for how long they must play. Entirely extempore music is insulting at any time during worship ("entirely" as distinct from rapidly planned) and these fellows could either prepare rough memoranda or, better still, play a piece by a decent composer. We cannot tell whether Wesley really was a great organist by international standards or whether he seemed so because others were bad. Why? Because he left no fine music for the organ or any other instrument. His pieces include some pleasant trifles and the *Choral Song and Fugue;* the tune of the *Choral Song* is like a strophe from a festal anthem that goes up like the rocket and comes down like the stick in a few seconds; unable to develop or extend it, Wesley repeats it between pedestrian episodes. The fugue wastes an attractive subject on a composition which is untidy, mismanaged and dull.

Most of his accompaniments are also dull despite the fact that he specified registration and set a notable example by ensuring that the pedals did not bumble from start to finish. He indicated where they were to be used and where not. Exceptionally careful is his accompaniment to *The Wilderness,* written on three staves and so imaginative that one wonders how fine a technician he would have been if he had been sent to study abroad and made to write independent orchestral parts to opera choruses, arias and scenas, as well as to compose overtures, string quartets and so on. He doubles voice parts to their detriment. See, for instance, the lovely opening treble solo of *Wash me throughly*; why double the boy's note in the second bar instead of letting all parts rest, and why include the C sharp which goes nowhere? What a pity that his organ parts do not sometimes overlap the choral entries and occasionally leave the voices unaccompanied!

Had there been anyone to train him in these matters and in the control of long-range pieces Sebastian Wesley might have been the anglican composer *par excellence.* His admirers declare that he is so, but he is not; he has left only one flawless piece, *Cast me not away*, and it is flawless because it is short enough to be conceived as a whole. This word-setting and vocal texture is not inferior to some of the best work of Byrd or Morley. (The organ part may be desirable for expressive purposes but it is unnecessary and may profitably be silenced for whole sections.) *Thou wilt keep him in perfect peace*, with its beautiful rise and fall of melody, bids fair at the opening to be another masterpiece, since the first transition to a texture for men's voices is excellent; but Wesley's constructional incompetence dogs him, and he ruins the piece by the faltering section "For thine is the kingdom".

Wesley is never vulgar, and if his pieces fail as wholes they have the magic of inspiration in many a section. What the voices meant to him and what the dignified declamation of words meant to him is shown in superb passages of recitative or arioso for unison voices, usually men's voices, where sections of prose would be ill-served by counterpoint or ponderous choral harmony. They may be introductory as at the opening of *Ascribe unto the Lord*, an anthem which can sound thrilling with a fine choir and instrument, or they may be transitional, as at "Being born again, not of corruptible seed" in *Blessed be the God and Father*—his most used anthem but far from his best because of the jejune final fugato.

Wesley consistently shows sensitivity not just to accentuation (which any dullard can observe) but to overtones and meanings of words and to his medium (boy-trebles and the interplay of cantoris and decani) and therefore his most beautiful passages are not only the result of sudden and special inspiration. At least a dozen are unforgettable, and he should be enrolled with artists and not merely with fine craftsmen. Beyond the skill and knowledge within his limited command there is the *tertium quid* which few of us possess but which we are fortunately able to recognise. Most of the units that make the arching sequences of *Wash me throughly* might come from a text book demonstration of suspensions—but not quite;

chromatics guide their tread unobtrusively in a way which nobody else of the period chose. Without advertisement Wesley achieves originality. Much of his work is well known and receives plenty of discussion in other books—the Walker-Westrup *History of Music in England*, Philips's *The Singing Church*, Fellowes's *English Cathedral Music* and so on. Here, however, the reader who doubts Wesley's artistry is asked to ponder the choice of each note and the syllable chosen for each note in the course of one of his inspired paragraphs. Ex. 17 merely provides material for this scrutiny from his patchy service in E (Morning, Communion and Evening settings). These basses and treatments of chords have no exact parallel although we wonder why not, so pedestrian might they seem to the untutored. Note the bass in the first extract and the spacing of chords as well as the pitch of separate notes in the second.[1]

Passages like these temper harsh judgment of Wesley's main weaknesses. One of them may be imputed to a condition forced upon him. Until 1832 it was not possible for him to play otherwise than ponderously when many stops were engaged or when manuals were coupled. If Bach could be nimble back in the eighteenth century why could not English players of the nineteenth? Explanation need not be long now that German and continental Bach-type tracker organs are being installed in high places, but one may emphasise the fact that *in England* the ascendant love of crescendo and diminuendo and of a wide range of tone colours led to the almost constant coupling of the swell organ to other manuals and to the further weighting of touch by the increase of stops; meanwhile proper pedaliers (not of German range) only gradually became attached to any but the larger instruments. To this day organs in most English churches are inadequate for the classical organ repertory unless the couplers to manuals are in constant use. In 1832 the Barker pneumatic action was

[1] It should be recorded that Wesley introduced the *St. Matthew Passion* to the "Three Choirs" at the Gloucester Festival of 1871.

S.S. Wesley: Magnificat in E

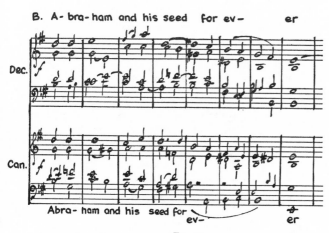

Ex. 17

patented; it could not have affected many organs before Wesley died, and most of his contemporaries spent their working lives with the heavy old instruments. In one Victorian work at least ponderosity is a positive virtue, suggesting unusual strength and magnificence in cathedral acoustics and with an organist who is not snobbishly given to accompanying everything as if it had been composed in Holland or Germany between 1650 and 1750.

This work is the splendid Evening Service in D minor by Thomas Attwood Walmisley, 1814–1856, professor of Music at Cambridge and simultaneously organist there at three colleges and Great St. Mary's to boot. Here are exactly those rapports between choir and organ, the "overlaps", the bars in which the organ is silent, that one longs for in Wesley. Here also, despite the sectional nature of canticle settings, is manifest an ability to "survey the whole" and that not merely by manipulation of themes; for we see it in both settings of *Gloria Patri*, said by Walmisley to use "a bass from Dumont". This acknowledgment explains much of the grandeur, for Walmisley's profession made him a connoisseur of old music, including that of the early seventeenth century when the scales were still used along with traces of the modes. It seems remarkable that a piece first heard (not before a musical antiquarian society) in the 1840s, should contain a passage like that in Ex. 18 yet proceed to the unaccompanied F major "He rememb'ring his mercy" in a minuet style that might have come from Attwood or Wesley. Walmisley had doubted if he should publish these canticles, and we look in vain for their equal among his other church pieces. The curious thing about *Walmisley in D minor* is that we do not find it merely curious, as we do "Strawberry Hill Gothick". Its liturgical effect is magnificent.

Walmisley was an able teacher and left good secular music. It must be remembered that if he had not died aged only forty-two he might have left more church music of the first class and rivalled the Oxford professor, Sir Frederick Gore

Ouseley, 1825–1889, in editing old music. The extraordinary quality of that D minor service could not have been achieved except by a more learned musician than the younger Wesley. Other church pieces by Walmisley, even the dignified service

Ex. 18

in B flat, represent not the professor but the workaday cathedral-type organist. In level of vitality they are comparable with the solid but not very distinguished works of Ouseley and Sir John Goss, 1800–1880. Ouseley's name is most respected for his scholarly work and his founding of Tenbury, and though Goss's church music is slightly more inventive than Ouseley's, Goss should also receive respect chiefly for his securing and maintaining reforms in singing and playing at St. Paul's. Our best native composer of their period, Sterndale Bennett (Walmisley's successor at Cambridge) did not distinguish himself as a church composer, though the unobtainable "Great is our Lord" is said to be finer than his simpering church pieces which are known. He directed the first English performance of the *St. Matthew Passion* in 1854 and, with Goldschmidt, edited *The Chorale Book for England* in 1863.

2. THE END OF THE CENTURY

There seems no point in examining music by the successors to these early Victorian musicians, for that very small part of it which is still respected is well enough known to most readers. No composer until Stanford rewards the exploration that leads to revival. There still exists a notion that we uphold the honour of a choir if we print "Anthem" or "Motet" on a service list and sing from open score, even if the piece has less textural interest than a Bach-harmonised chorale. Indeed a chorale, a mere plainsong hymn or a piece for one or two voices with organ continuo by some seventeenth century composer is more worth singing than *most* of the feebler English choral music from 1800 to the present day. If this seems harsh, let the reader answer two questions: (*a*) Apart from Stanford, what composer since 1800 supplied anglican eucharistic music that is worth singing or that clothes the rite instead of encumbering it? (*b*) How many of the pieces supplied in composite and popular volumes of anthems are musically as good as a decent hymn tune, popular song or dance? What a dreary load of rubbish we inflict on congregations for the very good reason that we need something more than congregational music with which to make choir practices varied and interesting! Yet there is the legacy of centuries to explore, the legacy of many countries as well as our own, and a copying machine is a better investment than multiple settings by *Jangler in G* or miserable anthems to Olde Englysshe words which only the singers can follow. How often do we see cathedral choirs singing from their own copies? Why, for instance, do we never hear Tomkins's splendid Fourth Service instead of a poorer one which happens to be in a publisher's book?

It is not for their music but to honour the men that mention is made of Henry Smart, 1813–1879, Sir Joseph Barnby, 1838–1896 and Sir John Stainer, 1840–1901, noting that neither of the first two held cathedral appointments though dozens of their pieces were used by cathedrals. Sullivan's church music is best forgotten; from it we can but illustrate only the nadir of sanctimonious vulgarity. Even that tune to a Christmas hymn might just as well be set to "John Gilpin was a citizen". Let us leave these composers until we are no longer concerned with cathedral music only.

PARRY

The last years of the century at last bring us two composers worth mention in general histories of music. The lives of Sir Hubert Parry, 1848–1918, and Sir Charles Villiers Stanford, 1852–1924, can be read elsewhere. As a composer Stanford was more nimble and versatile. Both studied in Germany and it is noteworthy that Stanford had two operas performed in Hamburg before he made his name here. Parry did not shine in opera, nor greatly in any instrumental music. He persisted in trying to write oratorios which lack dramatic vigour for all their effective patches, but he shone (at times even eclipsing Stanford) in two veins; the first was the grand manner which Elgar took over in orchestral pieces, the manner of Parry's *Blest Pair of Sirens*; the second was the serious but imaginative setting of words of philosophic and religious import for unaccompanied chorus, perhaps best exemplified in his *Songs of Farewell*. Some of the latter were called "Motets" by the composer and are used as church anthems. "Motet" was a misnomer if it was intended to mean anything more than "unaccompanied pieces to serious words", in which case one wonders why "part songs" was not sufficient unless Parry wanted to pay tribute to Bach or to older composers. (He does not do so stylistically although in some of his instrumental works, e.g. *Lady Radnor's Suite* for strings, there is a reversion to archaic design without deliberate archaism of melody and harmony.)

One of Parry's admirable characteristics, from his days at Eton onwards, was a tolerance of others' opinions along with unwillingness to reveal his own where this would hurt feelings. It was known that "honest Parry", like Brahms, remained agnostic on many points of doctrine then thought essential to churchmanship, yet he enjoyed public worship more than in merely admiring its liturgy, and it would be false to connect his small amount of first-rate church music with his agnosticism or with the fact that he did not hold or need to hold the organist's post at a cathedral. The truth is that only a tiny portion of any of Parry's music survives in general use. One wonders why he persisted in writing so much, for he was a very busy man with high ideals of service to students and institutions, and he was a painstaking writer and historian. (His book on Bach and his *Style of Music* still repay reading.)

With Parry, as with most men, virtues included limitations. Being at his best the master of glowing, slow-moving grandeur, as in his one superb anthem *I was glad* for the coronation of Edward VII in 1902, and also of tender, serious expression, he sounds ponderous when his limited genius is not in full control; he lacked Stanford's ready invention or musical wit that can make second-rate work attractive. For this reason his only organ pieces worth playing are the quiet preludes on popular hymn tunes or the exquisite little "Elegy" in *A Little Organ Book*; the noisy and ambitious chorale preludes lack fire, and the prelude and fugue named after his yacht "The Wanderer" bear their title all too appropriately; most of us would have preferred "The Adventurer". Cathedrals still/use the evening service *Parry in D*. One wonders why, for though of course the words are set carefully the music is merely respectable.

STANFORD

When we have grown up, passed through the mange of revulsion from our grandfathers' artistic expression, we shall see Stanford's operas, part-songs, solo songs and church music as better than those of any British composer between the seventeenth century and ours. The same claim cannot be made for his symphonies and orchestral rhapsodies, yet his assiduous application to chamber and instrumental music accounts for features of his church music which impart a vigour mistakenly called audacity. Foremost among these features are a long survey of design and its contributory survey of thematic paragraphing. I chose at Ex. 19B the final paragraph of a *Gloria in Excelsis* from one of his "complete" services, because in one of my appointments I had to play it once in every six Sundays, having taken over a scheme by which six settings were used in rotation except on certain fasts and feasts which had their special music. Thirty years later, having never sung that service nor heard it anywhere, and having been concerned only to play the organ part, not to teach it or rehearse it, I was able to go to a piano and play this and other passages. I found (as the reader will find) that the organ part alone makes satisfactory and purposeful music without the voices; in the example I have merely added the uppermost voice part after consulting the copy.

Incredibly enough, some of our church musicians have actually regarded as a fault the art which Stanford learnt from Wagner—not to write voice parts from verbal phrase to verbal phrase and then dull them with an accompaniment (as church composers had been doing since before S. S. Wesley) but to write a symphony, a total score, as Wagner did for each act of a drama, and give the voices a part in it.

Magnificat: Stanford

Ex. 19

If a conception is vocal, closely allied with verbal phrases, accents and intonations, why add the organ? Stanford does not, and in consequence some of his most superb pieces of church music revive—that is the word, although some of his predecessors occasionally wrote for unaccompanied voices— the art of "vocal scoring". A notable example is the Latin *Magnificat* of which Ex. 19A gives only a snippet. Among the finest Stanford anthems which some cathedrals have the good sense to use regularly are the two sets of three motets. *Beati*

Ex. 20

quorum via in the earlier set is unique in its symbolically regular rhythm, but it is sung *ad nauseam* because it appeals to timid choirmasters who doubt if anything merry or brilliant can be sacred. The brilliant eight-part *Coelos ascendit* is too infrequently heard and so is *Ye holy angels bright* in the later set. Fortunately *Glorious and powerful God* is less neglected. It is quoted at Ex. 20 to show Stanford's command of modulation not just for design in the broad but for telling passing effect.

Stanford's musical personality was distinct enough to be recognisable by manner and mannerism. Much has been made of his Dublin boyhood and his settings of traditional Irish verses and songs, and this was a rich enough source of melodic inspiration to dissatisfy him with tunes and turns of harmony that had become stale by overuse; but it would be dangerous to attribute to his birth in Ireland what may have come from his wide musical knowledge and his inventiveness. Most of his devotees will recognise his touch in the melody of Ex. 20A and also in the cadence, which happens to occur in one of Bach's harmonisations. (There can be no mistake, for it has a figured bass as well as Bach's "filling".) The point to emphasise is that Stanford knew more music, old and new, than most of his contemporaries. He edited *Purcell Society* volumes and unconsciously acquired vocabulary from Purcell. That cadence in Ex. 20A, like many another feature of his music, may be none the less idiomatic for being more the product of a well-stocked mind than of original experiment.

Stanford did not indulge in folksy sham-antiques, simulate the naïve, nor set words of antique spelling and syntax except with humorous intent—e.g. songs of the "Father O'Flynn" type. He disliked neo-modal mannerisms in his pupils and never attempted to do what Byrd or Gibbons had already done better. His attitude to word-setting can be summarised in the belief that innocuous regard for speech is valueless without marriage to music that would be fine without the text. On this subject his little book *Musical Composition* draws from Brahms's songs the lessons to be learnt by church composers. Stanford's was not the mere love of declamation shown by amateurs to Monteverdi, who knew the popular complaint against *il tedio del recitativo* which we ought to raise again in our day. Stanford was so sensitive to the singer's art that he upheld the Palestrinian practice of using the upward leap of a minor sixth but avoiding that of the major sixth, which choirs rarely sing in tune. He understood phonetic phenomena as they affect singers.[1] The same feeling for medium is shown in Stanford's organ works, even the less attractive ones like

---

[1] As Beethoven did not. Except with bad singers Beethoven's high notes make no extraordinary demand by their pitch. If choirboys cannot sing without strain a chromatic scale which goes two or three notes beyond their 'top

the *Sonata Britannica*. It is hardly a compliment to say that he has left the average organist more short pieces that are really useful and worth playing than has any other British composer, for how many composers of any nation have left us even Stanford's twenty or so that can be so described? They are not all contained in the two albums of *Six Pieces* and it is time all his organ works were issued together. The clean lines and harmonies, the unpretentious yet interesting textures of little voluntaries like "On a Theme of Orlando Gibbons", or "On an Irish Church Melody", "Trio", or "Marcia Eroica" are shining examples among the pretentious and jejune organ pieces of his day and ours.

Yet as we shall note when we look at parish church music, organists and choirs of moderate ability were hardly to blame for using what they could manage, taking it from inferior composers when better ones failed them. Undoubtedly much of the inferior music was a means of devotion and a stepping stone to better music. I do not believe that it corrupted taste. The old fool who chides boys for reading *Deadwood Dick* or whatever has now supplanted it in favourite juvenile fiction should be told that a boy who reads "bloods" may come to read *Macbeth* and recognise that horror, pity and the rest are more powerfully expressed than in his earlier fiction, whereas it is certain that the boy who reads nothing will not. From Smart and Stainer to Bach; from Stanford very much sooner to Bach and to Purcell.

THE CATHEDRAL LEGACY

Let anyone who would absolutely condemn the twopence-coloured music of the nineteenth century remember that

---

A', they deserve smack or sack. Beethoven's incompetence lay in asking for a series of syllables on the unchanged high note. (Alas, it always *is* changed, not always by loss of general pitch, but by ugly retchings between syllables!) The vocal mechanism being tensed for the high note, change of vowel or consonant meets resistance.

cathedral and church were thronged with more, if not more discreet, musical pilgrims than before. Today they have records and broadcasts, to say nothing of concerts and opera in the bigger cities, and they are not dependent upon organists to know the classics by arrangements, as I first came to know Wagner at Lemare's recitals. Both choir and organ music seemed more interesting than it does now, for today's organists cannot easily lighten programmes and let the great classics of the instrument stand out as does a Beethoven sonata or a set of Brahms variations in a piano recital which includes some Chopin studies or Schumann genre pieces; and if choirs use only such music of English provenance as is worthy to stand by the best music intended for the Roman or Lutheran Church there will be few days in the year when services or anthems come from any period outside 1580 to 1690. Indeed it would be well for our choral foundations if they forced themselves for six months or longer to use nothing that was expressly composed for them by British musicians; the best British church music would shine better if it were not in one room of a historical museum with poorish specimens of its own kind crowding it.

Social and economic conditions of the Victorian epoch enabled cathedral employees to live (while it was still fashionable to learn singing and piano playing) on a lay-clerk's stipend, and most citizens of a small city could work near their homes and depend little on public transport. Cathedrals could carry out the reforms which the evangelical and tractarian movements had laid upon the conscience of churchmen, and the buying power of money as well as the lowness of wages accounted for restorations of buildings, organs and schools. The daily services, far more of them choral than they are now, were more zealously performed at the end of the nineteenth century than at any time since the Laudian period in the seventeenth. Many of my older readers must have heard their elders speaking of excellent music at this or that provincial cathedral, and the average musical Briton, not widely travelled, regarded an outstanding local church musician with awe. My choirmaster and his friends spoke of "Bennett of Lincoln", "Noble of York", "Keeton of Peterborough", "Daddy Mann of King's", "South of Sarum", "Brewer of Gloucester" and so on. When I was old enough to visit places where these worthies still presided I was also old enough to know that their day was over and that my generation sought different ideals—not better but different. The trouble is that reform is too often an event, a revolution of a few decades, instead of a permanent policy. Schools modelled upon Rugby long after Arnold was dead became little philistine hells which would have horrified a new Arnold, and despite a published report on the reform of cathedrals and chapters our older choral foundations (I am not speaking of "parish church cathedrals" like Southwark, Portsmouth, Newcastle, etc.) are only slowly tackling new demands in boys' education; and despite the theory we read in guide books they are not *genuinely* bishops' churches or diocesan centres. They are too often no more than reformed Barchesters, and the better musicians who serve them find themselves straining for "special" occasions because the routine is moribund, neither glorifying God nor inspiring men.

Why mention this in connection with the nineteenth century? Because the very reforms of the nineteenth century have imposed a burden on the cathedrals as on the parish churches. Times of service are still inadequately adjusted to the employment of lay clerks, the educational demands upon boys' time or the attraction of worshippers. To muddle on, chapters have curtailed the number of choral services, but have made much of the idea of poorly attended daily services as being a continuation of the monastic *opus Dei*. This is false. A monk's whole profession was *opus Dei*. He maintained the performance not of one or two choir offices, but of an incessant cycle from Prime to Compline grouped round the main service—Mass. Paid minstrels and paid canons singing *one* choir office on certain days of the week, and that office

Evening Prayer (before tea and with six hours to go until retirement to bed) provide but a forced resemblance to *opus Dei*. However splendid the music (and in at least six cathedrals as I write the music is most creditably maintained), our older cathedrals must either become museums of music written for them since the Reformation or they must completely "rethink" their daily and Sunday time-tables, not scorning congregational music and popular services, yet making sure that by serving the needs of a diocesan centre and a "bishop's church" (the bishop should live on the spot) they can also maintain the purely choir service of cathedral tradition. If instead of trimming from an inherited reform our cathedrals could continue with an unceasing reform they would not lose their choral inheritance; the more healthy state of their worship would make the traditional service more effective.

The last thing to be said about nineteenth century British cathedrals is that they moved to high standards of singing and playing even though some of the music was pretentious and windy. Ours is more often pretentious and sour, as it ought to be when there is little radiance of faith.

CHOIRS IN PARISH CHURCHES

Parish music in the years just after Victoria's accession was generally worse than when Sir Roger de Coverley engaged an itinerant choirmaster. Many churches had no instrumental aid to singing—a happy state of affairs which one would like to see enforced today at least during Advent and Lent; it would give organists time to practise and study other music than the organ repertory, and it would show congregations how snobbish and lazy they are, as compared with the full-throated peasants of Bavaria and Italy. They are snobbish because they regard parish choirs as servants who will do their singing for them while they mumble, looking up and down from books like hens drinking; they are lazy because they will not even breathe or speak decently. I know of one incumbent who had to face an irate church council because he insisted that the congregation stood ready to sing the first word as soon as it heard the tune played over. Oh no! That was lowering themselves to the mere status of the choir, the servants! How pleasant, during a recent visit to Ulster, to hear congregations pronounce a hearty AYMEN to prayers!

Early in the nineteenth century churches which could muster only one instrument very sensibly used a violone (or double bass), a bassoon, cello or trombone.[1] On the continent competent and well-balanced little bands could be found in town churches where the players served during the week in theatres or dance rooms, but in the British Isles incumbents would hardly have made the barrel-organ almost ubiquitous in country churches during the early nineteenth century if gallery minstrels could have provided reliable and satisfying harmony to enough tunes; after all the largest barrel-organs (those with three barrels) provided only three dozen tunes. When I played the organ at Bideford during the first world war an old lady told me she remembered "two organs before this one. The first played six tunes; and we were told to bring a pencil to church on some Sunday afternoons (service in winter was at 3.00 p.m.) so that after sermon we could write out the words of hymns on the fly-leaves of our Prayer Books. I had to gum some leaves with hymns into mine. The Rector dictated 'Sun of my Soul' from Mr. Keble's book and 'Lead kindly Light', and people didn't altogether like this . . . especially those who could not write. Some said the Rector was an old Pusey and some said he was a Methody. In those days we had no choir stalls but the children sang from the side gallery."

Until the middle of the nineteenth century, as we are

---

[1] Two pleasant and valuable accounts of instruments in English parish churches are Canon K. H. Macdermott's *The Old Church Gallery Minstrels* (S.P.C.K. 1948) and Canon Noel Boston's *The Barrel-Organ Book* (Boston and Langwill, 19 Melville Street, Edinburgh 3).

sometimes reminded in novels as late as Hardy's, there persisted in the Established Church of England, Wales and Ireland (not until later in Scotland, where the episcopal church was not the established one) a very clear contrast between two types of worship which had been distinct since the Reformation—that of collegiate bodies, including not just the old cathedrals but also certain college chapels at Oxford and Cambridge and such royal peculiars as St. George's, Windsor and Westminster Abbey, and that of parish or other churches which had no choral foundations. Some churches, including many dissenting churches, had choirs to lead the metrical psalmody or, where Methodism had left its impact, hymnody with occasional pieces of choir music. Such choirs were not founded and provided for by statute, and were not what the compilers of the Prayer Book had in mind when they inserted the rubric "In quires and places where they sing here followeth the anthem", or "Then the clerks shall sing the following". The Reformation settlement made no specific provision for music in parish churches. Various rubrics of the B.C.P. containing the phrase "said or sung" suggest the continuance of local customs which required no regulation. All shades of anglican churchmanship have since been grateful that an age supposedly less tolerant than our own had the good sense *not* to fill the cracks with precise rubrics and regulations, but to leave much to local custom and interpretation provided that all was said and done "decently and in order".

The Prayer Book made no mention of hymns, yet we know that they were customary in some churches because a clause in Elizabeth I's *Injunctions* of 1559, which still appears as a rubric in the Prayer Book of the American Episcopal Church, reads thus: "In the beginning or in the end of Common Prayer, there may be sung an hymn or such like song to the praise of Almighty God, in the best sort of melody and music that may be conveniently devised." This could have been quoted against later objections to "human hymns" as distinct from metrical psalms. It also supports the practice of singing first and then inconsistently reaching the words "O Lord open thou our lips". Clergy may use the Prayer Book with considerable freedom and still claim to have kept their promise to "use the services of the said Book and none other". As has just been shown, they may be loyal and still make nonsense of the ritual when they alter its *order*.

Before the Education Act of 1870 widespread illiteracy limited the parish repertory; the few metrical psalms and hymns were still "lined out" by the parish clerk who thus reminded people without books of the forthcoming words. The musical effect is scarcely conceivable to modern imagination, and it must have prevented the sensitive from attending any services except those which were said. At least they were spared today's incessant and often incompetent organ playing, for few parish churches had organs. Their bass viols, clarinets, serpents or bassoons were silent except when they were actually supporting psalms or hymns. It may be asked why parish churches are mentioned at all in a chapter on choral music. The answer should be obvious: it is because today, thanks to the nineteenth century, "choral music" and "choirs and places where they sing", no longer refers solely to the choral foundation.

The awakening of the 1830s, following the Oxford and Cambridge zealots whom I call the Tractarians for want of a more accurate designation, brought into the smallest country church an ideal of public worship derived from several older ones—that of the Methodists, the Roman Catholics, the reformed cathedrals and even the monks who had used those greater churches before they were turned into English cathedrals.[1] In time ugly protruding organs and choir stalls, to

[1] A characteristic of most English cathedrals before the twentieth century is that they were formerly "minsters" or monastery churches. Unlike the great French cathedrals which rise from market squares and shops and betoken civic pride in bishop and diocese, they are still set in green precincts near streams that served for the mill and laundry, as well as for fish, and most of them still have their cloisters, libraries, refectories, infirmaries and schools. Inside they

say nothing of encaustic tiles, oak panelling, alabaster rere-doses, stained glass, fald stools and the whole tawdry clutter of Pre-Raphaelite bric-à-brac filled tiny Norman sanctuaries and completed the crowding that had begun when naves were pewed and galleried to the last square yard. Yet the new furnishing was done in piety. "The House of the Lord shall be exceeding magnifical" was quoted by the reformers, and humble folk loved the marmoreal and wrought-iron magnificence which only the wealthy had in private houses.

The musical parallel to this was the introduction of choirs to chant psalmody in cathedral style or to "Gregorians", their attendance in many parish churches on red-letter weekdays, the bawling of canticles to *Jangler in G* and *Crasher in C*, of anthems by cathedral composers and, following Methodist practice, from oratorios. Desiring the elaboration where resources were naïve or limited, the humbler churches bought settings from the ever-flowing pen of Mr. Caleb Simper. Eucharistic music was sung either to Merbecke harmonised by Stainer, or to Englished popular masses, or to music by dozens of astute purveyors who had no more to say musically than Mr. Simper but said it with more rhetoric. There were sung litanies, sung responsories, sung prayers, even sung creeds and sung Lord's Prayers. Even this was not enough and still is not enough for some. Where this ridiculous hubbub is still loved there are musical walks in and out of service called processions or recessions, *Nunc dimittis* may be stuck on the end of the Communion rite, evening services are dragged out past their appointed conclusion by vesper hymns, sung vestry prayers are turned into public devotions, and the organ will make sure that the one means of worship never to be enjoyed is silence. Ask an organist why we may not observe the solemn days of Passion-

---

may retain the big screen or pulpitum, with organ surmounting, that cuts off the monks' choir. St. Paul's and York were civic, not monastic. Thus "York Minster" and "Durham Cathedral" are misnomers. Durham was a minster; York never had a monastic community at its cathedral of St. Peter.

tide by the good old custom of walking in without his churnings. Ask him why he churns, with his 16 foot pedal bumbling away, during the Communion of the People. Ask him why he cannot play a chorale prelude and then SHUT UP, and ten to one he will say that he and the people find "the pattering of feet" eerie. Oh yes, that is understandable in our day of fidgets, when the radio must be kept on all day because of our dread of being left alone with our empty minds; but in church the disease is a relic of the day when any unadorned corner at home or in church was thought to be a reproach. The great word was "introduce", and it was matter for congratulation if something could be introduced in defiance of a cautious or opposing bishop.

There was a certain amount of lay opposition to some introductions, and significantly enough it was at first levelled against the very garment that had formerly distinguished cathedral from parish worship—the surplice, the choir dress which had formerly been worn only by clergy in parish churches and then only for the administration of sacraments, not for reading and preaching. There were "surplice riots", objecting to this garment in the pulpit and stalls of parish churches, and I wish they had been successful.[1] Again, if reform had been a steady continuous policy instead of a twenty-year crescendo which became so paralysed that in many churches service today is almost exactly as it was a century ago (without the gusto) we should have wholly benefited from the changes though we should use little of the music sung at the time. Of course parish choirs are to be encouraged, if only because it is better for young people to do things regularly than be regularly harangued as passive auditors, if they will submit. As Nicholson, founder of the Royal School of Church Music, tirelessly repeated, "The

---

[1] Though I am a stiff high churchman I wonder why low churchmen do not insist on preaching and reading the choir offices in a gown so that Holy Communion may receive the distinction once accorded to a rite of divine institution.

choirboys of today are the churchmen of tomorrow", to which in a cynical age we may add "At least we hope many are". We shall err even more from the strict path of history, however, if we discuss the pros and cons of choir music in parish services, the good things and the abuses that followed the Victorian change in those services, for most denominations are now embroiled in proposals for further and drastic changes in the patterns of worship.

The change of pattern which swept across the British Isles in the 1830s and 1840s began at a little parish church in Coleraine, where the vicar, John Jebb, born in Dublin in 1805, had come to love the choral service as a schoolboy at Winchester and an undergraduate at Trinity College, Dublin. There could have been no suspicion that he followed the Tractarians since he took this first parish (and that in remote Ireland) before a single "Tract for the Times" had been published and before the Cambridge high churchmen had become interested in the externals of public worship. Jebb simply liked music and did not intend losing it when he was rusticated by his incumbency. He still held it in 1832 when given a prebendal stall at Limerick Cathedral, but he moved to Hereford in 1843, gave and published lectures on church music, restored Tudor settings of responses and litanies which had been corrupted in harmony and rhythm, published a catalogue of the fine Peterhouse music library in Cambridge which had been much enriched in the Laudian period when Cosin was Master of that college, and edited several old works which include settings and anthems by Caustun. Jebb thought it would be pleasant in his rural retreat to train a few voices which would join his. He then let people in the parish and locality hear some of the delights offered "in quires and places where they sing". They sampled them with relish, first in the schoolroom and then, outside service time, in the church. Linen being an Irish product and inexpensive in that area, choir robes were made by proud parents of the boys who had been taught sight-reading and voice production, or by the wives or friends of the men; and on some Sunday in 1834 (the exact date is not yet known) for the first time since the Reformation if not in British history, a parish choir walked surpliced into pews that had been arranged college-wise behind the reading desk and led parish worship with the imitation-cathedral trimmings that are ubiquitously familiar to us.

It is incorrect to say, therefore, that sympathy with one shade of reforming churchmanship initiated the parish choral service or its adoption in other parishes after Jebb's, especially since few areas are more strongly Protestant than Northern Ireland. Evangelicals as well as Tractarians welcomed this particular change, partly because the Methodists (now Dissenters and no longer high Anglicans) had made musical inroads upon the anachronistic and comatose services caricatured in Hogarth's prints and partly for reasons which make us today unwilling to disband choirs which do not rehearse properly or attend as regularly as they should, are easy neither upon the eye nor the ear, and sing only what could be managed by the congregation.

Considerable influence upon the movement for parish choirs came from Tractarian centres like the Margaret Chapel, replaced by Butterfield's All Saints, Margaret Street, and equipped with a choir school;[1] but earlier in the century Leeds parish church was more generally influential than any London "society" church. Air raids, slum clearance, traffic control and the movement of population away from the centre of the city have combined to make today's visitor

---

[1] Several London churches had either choir schools or coveted scholarships for choristers as late as the 1920s when my choirmaster used to take us to hear them sing on Saturdays, showing us other sights of London before or after service. We were particular to note the behaviour and singing of the boys at St. Andrews, Wells Street, rivals to the Margaret St. boys just round the corner. This church declined immediately it disbanded its choir school and has been demolished. Other famous choirs were Holy Trinity, Sloane St., St. Peter's, Eaton Square, St. George's, Hanover Square, and St. Mary Magdalene, Paddington, where the boys had been trained under Redhead's redoubtable discipline.

regard Leeds Parish Church as an insulated building like a provincial cathedral, except that its precincts are of paving stones instead of grass. Its heavy Victorian galleries and pews, yielding to a theatrically colourful Tractarian apse and sanctuary, transport one into the days of Dickens, and it is no fault of a succession of good clergy (for Leeds Parish Church is still a very live missionary centre) that on some days the building, though rarely deserted, seems only a monument to its great past. In its famous days it rose from one of the most populous areas of the city and had been specially favoured by the Wesleys in their missions to the north. Just after the first impact of the Tractarian movement at the end of the 1830s its most famous vicar, later Bishop Hook, planned to enlarge it and rebuild it, and to provide it with parish schools and amenities that would make it a mission centre more effective in a great industrial city than any ancient English cathedral had ever been. Its music should be both hearty in the Methodist sense and also fine artistically. Hook consulted Jebb and set up not merely a surpliced parish choir but a system of payment to both boys and lay clerks, and it was not for the modest financial reward alone that competition for a place in the stalls was greater than in any ancient cathedral. Leeds had a better choir than most cathedrals, for Hook secured as its organist and trainer the most famous of all English church musicians, S. S. Wesley. This was the first parish church at which the daily offices were sung by a permanent choir which was augmented on Sundays. The Sunday services achieved an admirable mixture of congregational and choir participation and became models to be copied far and wide.

"Good was it in that dawn to be alive", in slum church, residential-area church or country church, and good it remained for the whole century whether the music was carefully sung or whether, as in most places, the psalms were punished with a thump at the "bar line" and a fast bowler's accelerando to that heavily marked wicket. Oh the thrill when "our" solo boys and choir could pull off one of the "Wildernesses", Wesley's or Goss's, or Mendelssohn's "Hear my prayer" complete with "O for the wings of a dove"! And how early one had to arrive to be sure of a seat (in the "free" aisles) for the Lent cantata or the harvest anthem or the Palm Sunday or Good Friday performance of Stainer's *Crucifixion*! It has already been pointed out that several of the popular composers of late Victorian choir music were not in cathedral appointments and hoped rather than expected that their settings would enter cathedral lists. Some deserved this, for instance the vigorous, unsentimental but not very subtle Henry Smart, whose lengthy service in B flat achieves a ceremonial grandeur with its passages for the trumpet or tuba stop, and whose F major *Te Deum*, for all the constant four-bar phrases, is clean, dignified and tuneful; many congregations must have joined in some of its phrases since in many churches it has been, and is, the usual "stand by" for occasions of thanksgiving.

To praise the spirit of an age is not to ask for a revival of the music which expressed that spirit. We should not bring back the gusto without being false to ourselves, nor could we bring it back without the sentimentality and theatricality which went with it. The shallowness of most late nineteenth century church music is typified in the finest scholar and Bach player among its composers—Sir John Stainer. Had Stainer been born a Parisian or a Viennese his facile melodic gift and command of harmony could have made him a witty rival to Offenbach, Johann Strauss, Lecocq or Planquette. Look again at such "ariettes" as "King ever glorious" in *The Crucifixion* and note the theatre orchestra (wood-wind triplets, pizzicato basses, trombone choruses and so on) implicit in the organ accompaniment, and the operetta-like nature of the vocal line. The words of that item should be "O ma Dalila!" If we can forget the vulgar words added to the biblical ones and imagine this "devotion" to be theatre music, we shall recognise it as attractive and inventive in place after place, from the opening chorus "Could ye not watch" to the decidedly effective setting for unaccompanied male voices of the Seven Words. Do not let us underestimate Stainer. We ought to have sent most of his church music to be pulped, and let us waste no time in delaying the pulping. And if Stainer's goes, then let most choir music by his contemporaries and inferiors precede it. Not much is worth saving before the best of Stanford's.

6

Music in the Free Churches

From Shakespeare onwards we are made aware that people who have called themselves "C. of E." have throughout the centuries to our own either envied or derided the enthusiastic psalm-singing or hymn-singing of dissenters, who included members of a protestant community which, from its inception restricted music in their worship—the Society of Friends, commonly called Quakers. Since Quakers have become opera conductors and promoters of concerts, since they are also noted for a gentle and wide tolerance of other people's beliefs and for a love of the arts, people have questioned their association with puritanism. During the seventeenth century they undoubtedly upheld a puritan distrust of luxury, including music that went with dancing, the theatre and popular entertainment; but it was not for the reasons that silenced church music under the Commonwealth that they excluded music from their main worship, called "The Meeting". They banned it from The Meeting because "set forms" were to have no place therein, and music was undoubtedly composed in "set forms". So were verses for that matter.

Quaker life and thought became less austere during the eighteenth century. The nineteenth saw the foundation of Quaker schools wherein the young were treated with kindly understanding of individuals and a liberal attitude towards the arts, sciences and games. Music was not just a "subject" but had a place in school assemblies. These were not replicas of The Meeting for they included hymns, songs and anthems.

Quakers were also foremost in encouraging their young folk to hear purely instrumental music, to participate in it, and to love music to fine words (whether thoroughly secular poetry or of some moral or religious trend) as an occupation akin to spiritual contemplation. The schools did their part to make each successive generation of Quakers more liberal than the last if not more sophisticated. Before the nineteenth century was finished, although the adult Sunday morning Meeting continued loyal to tradition, and has never used music, another kind of assembly, called the "Evening Meeting" grew frequent. Though regarded as a religious observance it is less fixed and formal in its contents than any other service. It may include prayer, commentary or discussion, the hearing of music, the singing of hymns and readings from scripture or from other sources. These include plays and books not readily associated with religion, but the tendency of Evening Meetings is certainly philosophic.

Thus, though Quakers have written the words and tunes of hymns there has emerged no such entity as a characteristic Quaker contribution to church music. Quakers are free to attend the worship of other churches and to join or hear their music. When they sing or listen at their assemblies (other than The Meeting) they show less prejudice than any other Christian sect. They avail themselves of hymns and choir music composed for other denominations and they hear music from secular sources. I do not know if one could have heard at any nineteenth century Meeting of the Friends, as I have done in the Euston Road, Handel violin sonatas and Latin motets; but it was during the nineteenth century that the Friends became most widely associated with liberal thought, practical philanthropy at home and abroad, progressive educational ideas and love of the arts.

Though I could not conscientiously embrace certain essential Quaker beliefs and practices I have wilfully written about their attitude to music because almost all the effete, affected or downright bad compositions written for churches derive their feebleness from the infertility of a narrow, over-worked field of inspiration. In short they are churchy and sectarian, and the Quakers have never been so, nor produced churchy art. Even the best of early Victorian anglican composers, S. S. Wesley, might have been a better one if he had not composed exclusively for the church. His father was his superior simply because he wrote secular music.

CALVINISTIC CHURCHES

The present claims of some churches to be Calvinistic, whatever they were once, are as amusing to the musician as to the theologian. I have enjoyed hearing both Mozart's and Fauré's settings of the Requiem Mass (not of course at a Celebration!) in churches of Calvinistic allegiance, though I doubt if I should have heard Latin there before our own century. No church can claim to observe Calvin's own style of worship unless its Sunday morning service is eucharistic[1] and unless it allows no other music than the unharmonised singing of scriptural words, chiefly metrical psalms and canticles. Despite the more sour preachers and legislators in Cromwell's Britain, there is no warrant for the supposition that Calvinism incurs a distaste for secular music. Its adherents notably cultivated chamber music during the Commonwealth and, like the Lutherans, printed music for the pious family circle. According to Schweitzer the six years Bach spent at the reformed or Calvinised court of Cöthen were the most pleasant in his career; certainly they were those in which he came to know many Italian sonatas and concertos, French suites and overtures, theatre and concert music, which helped his brilliant Lutheran church music to transcend that of the organists

[1] Calvin found that the burghers of Switzerland did not like preparing for and receiving Holy Communion every Sunday. He therefore modified the morning service but arranged that a full Celebration took place in one church when it did not in the next. The Lutheran morning service remained ceremoniously eucharistic until Bach's time, Leipzig being the last stronghold of Orthodoxy to cede to Pietism in 1770.

and cantors to whom he was first indebted. As an Orthodox or high Lutheran Bach disliked the court chapel which he called "an unlovely vault", but let us note that when it changed to the Pietist regime it did not silence or dismantle its organ. Unlike the Protestants of Switzerland, France and Scotland, the court of Cöthen did not forgo its organ-accompanied hymns and chorales for a rigid fare of metrical psalms.

Dutch Protestants had allowed organs in churches during the seventeenth century, but the wretched Louis Bourgeois was imprisoned in Calvin's Geneva for issuing his lovely settings of Marot's vernacular psalms with vocal harmonies. The Goudimel and Bourgeois tunes which are so admired among our standard hymns were originally published in Lyons. Very few places allowed the ban on vocal harmonies to outlast Calvin himself, though in Scotland, Wales and America the dislike of organs remained until the nineteenth century.[1]

We may wonder why organs and other hymns than the "foundation" metrical psalms crept into continental Calvinism before and during the nineteenth century while they were still bitterly opposed in Scotland, so much farther away from Geneva, "the protestant Rome". Surely the reason is that continental Calvinists (except in France, where they remained strict even after the Revolution) were influenced by Pietist Lutherans among their compatriots and German neighbours. The "second reformation", the final yielding of Orthodox Lutheranism to Pietism, was complete by about 1765, but Lutheran churches retained the fine organs of which

---

[1] Calvin was not, like Luther, a musician and notable music-lover, but a great theologian. He himself did not display his followers' fanatical distrust of music but merely wished *the words* of Holy Writ to be sung plainly, and to avoid the practices of the Roman Church which required the professional cultivation of music. It has been wondered that Calvin did not favour the singing to plainchant of the psalms and other scriptural prose, which was closer to Holy Writ than the popular verse form; but plainsong, especially with antiphonal chanting, was probably rejected because of its monkish associations. Zwingli at Zurich banned music totally from worship.

Germany and Holland were so justly proud. They no longer kept the church orchestras, cantatas and elaborate eucharistic music known to Bach. The former boys' choirs disappeared and the schools became ordinary *Gymnasia*, corresponding with English grammar schools; but Lutherans continued with mixed choirs to lead the hymns and simple responses. By the nineteenth century continental protestant services showed very little sectarian difference in their music, and they had much hymnody in common.

SCOTLAND

In Scotland, according to Dr. Percy Scholes,[1] himself a Calvinist, organs were not common after the Reformation "until near the end of the nineteenth century" when "organists had largely to be attracted from Anglican and other churches in the north of England by high salaries".[2] (Organists are still better paid in Scotland than elsewhere in Great Britain.) In the two decades following 1860 a flood of lucubrations for or against organs appeared in Scottish cities. Some of them quoted such Old Testment phrases as "Praise him upon the strings and pipe", and others averred that there was "a de'il in every pipe"—even in a precentor's pitch pipe. Scholes gives the following dates for "official permission" to erect organs: Established Kirk 1866: United Presbyterians 1872: Free Church 1883. He reminds us, too, of the munificence of Andrew Carnegie after he had become a millionaire in the New World, but this cannot have caused any great impetus to organ building until the turn of the century.

Perhaps because of its limitations Calvinism made a distinct contribution to church music until the end of the seventeenth century; it then ceased to be distinctive. I have suggested

[1] P. A. Scholes, *The Puritans and Music*, Oxford, 1934 and *The Oxford Companion to Music*, London, 1938.

[2] The first protestant church in the city of Edinburgh to install an organ was Augustine (now Augustine-Bristo) Congregational Church, in 1863. The first parish church in that city to do so was the Kirk of Greyfriars, in 1865.

why this was so in Switzerland. Dr. Millar Patrick's affection-
ate study[1] amply documents the gradual loss of distinction
in Scotland and America which came about for similar reasons.
We may accept Patrick's strong censure of the eighteenth
century wherein many churches used only five of the twelve
tunes printed in 1666 as survivors from the wonderful *Scottish
Psalter* of 1635, known to us through Sir Richard Terry's
facsimile edition of 1935. How little the fine old tunes and
virile harmonies meant to Presbyterians as late as 1864 may
be judged by the fact that when, in that year, William Ewing
of Glasgow produced at his own expense the complete Psalter
that had been laboriously edited from old sources by Dr.
Neil Livingston, Minister of Stair by Ayr, only a few scholars
bought it; churches did not want it. The choir-led congregations in the first half of the nineteenth century used the
following music:

1. A mere handful of the old psalm tunes.

2. Tunes set to psalms and paraphrases[2] in the old metres,
but composed late in the eighteenth century or early in the
nineteenth and influenced by Methodist hymnody. Quotation
is not needed to show the change from old rugged modality
to "hymn" progressions, which we find in the well-known
Martyrdom (sung to "As pants the hart" or to "O God of
Bethel" in today's English collections and to Psalm 130 in
Scotland), and in *Stracathro* (*E. H.* 445). One does not dis-
parage such tunes, for they have survived too hardily to lack
a strength which was less evident when they were prettified
by the appoggiaturas and other embellishments of their time.
Some of their companions are less admirable, and but for

---

[1] Millar Patrick, *Four Centuries of Scottish Psalmody*, Oxford, 1949.

[2] Certain Scottish churches supplemented psalms by metrical paraphrases of
passages from Scripture in the middle of the eighteenth century. The practice
was officially authorised in 1781. The authorisation of other hymns was not
general until past the middle of the nineteenth century; but they were used in
many churches before then. This makes close parallel with Anglican churches
which used various local hymn collections until the publication of *A. and M.*
in 1861.

their metres and association with metrical psalmody would be recognised as sounding no indigenous note. An example is *Crimond* (first published in 1872) which, since its popularisation by use at a royal wedding, has been requested for weddings, funerals, baptisms and all kinds of services, since the doggerel to which it is allied (perhaps the poorest surviving version of the 23rd psalm) spares agnostic mourners, wedding guests and other gatherers the mention of specifically Christian beliefs. The tune is a competent assembly of reach-me-down phrases. Every two bars could be shown to correspond with the musical small change of minuets and other pieces of the Mozart period. It is not a bad tune, but it does not deserve its place at the top of the pops.

3. A type of tune new to Scotland but not to British Methodists. I call it the "Ilkley Moor" chorusy-type, more hearty and less heart-felt than the type *Martyrdom* represents. It it said to have owed much to Methodist admiration of oratorio choruses, with their "vocal scoring"—alternate upper and lower voices and fugued entries. Not all these "old Methodist tunes" are jejune, but none could be mistaken for Handel's. They were popular at Methodist "gala" meetings in which instruments joined big numbers of voices. Wesley himself disliked fugal sections which obscured the verbal syntax in effects which have often been humorously parodied. Tovey was fond of quoting "And catch this flee—And catch this fleeting breath". The source may be apocryphal, but not that of "Bring down Sal—Bring down Salvation from on high", which I sang as a boy at Sunday School festivals. To avoid censure, Methodist composers often left the "fuguing" to doxologies and final Hallelujahs. In Scotland several tunes of this style emanated from St. George's Kirk in Edinburgh through the collaboration of a musical Minister, Dr. Andrew Thomson, and his precentor,[1] R. A. Smith, who had been

---

[1] The Precentor's office was in some places a sinecure, though he might be used like the English parish clerk for the "lining out" of psalms and paraphrases. As in England, too, the precentor was often the local schoolmaster

a choirmaster in Reading but went to Paisley as a weaver
c. 1800. Thomson's own tunes are amateurish, the harmony
being particularly crude. Ex. 21 shows part of his tune to
Psalm 148, which is more mildly "chorusy" than others by him
which repeat lines (or add Hallelujahs) for enjoyment of the
antiphony between upper and lower voices, and between
one, two, or three parts and all four. His most famous tune
now is "St. George's, Edinburgh", sung to Psalm 24 verses
7–10 (Scottish Psalter, 190).

Ex. 21

Other hymns than psalms and paraphrases were locally
and occasionally used before the middle of the century, when
they were distinguished from authorised Presbyterian music
by being called "human hymns". They first creep into collections of psalm tunes as "Evening Hymn", "Easter Hymn",
etc., and no doubt their presence was first explained as making
them available for use on domestic and social occasions. An
example is "Christmas Hymn"—John Byrom's "Christians
awake" to the familiar tune *Yorkshire*. The style is "chorusy"
or "old Methodist", and I am told that in parts of north
England the last line is still sung first by sopranos and altos
and then repeated "full". The name *Yorkshire* is questionable
since its composer, John Wainwright, was at Manchester
Collegiate Church, and its general use began at Stockport
Parish Church in 1750. But both this and "human hymns"
dating from the nineteenth century itself did not generally

---

and his choir the children. Many of the best precentors had come from over
the border and, in the nineteenth century, became keen teachers of sight
singing by so-fa, which appeared in psalm and hymn books.

invade kirk music until their demand in anglican churches expedited the publication of *A. and M.* Part of their attraction both north and south of the border must have been (*a*) their metrical variety which afforded contrast with the constant C.M. and S.M. of psalms and paraphrases (*b*) the relief of contemporary poetic language after the stylised diction and rime-seeking that produced

> A stubborn and a froward heart
> Depart quite from me shall,

LUTHERANS

The Lutheran hymns of the late eighteenth and nineteenth centuries were all too human, and all too influential upon the compilers of British collections, including *A. and M.*, despite the fact that Catherine Winkworth's valuable *Chorale Book for England* was not published till 1863; it was concerned, however, with the old chorales. Once when I was sitting by Geoffrey Shaw at the organ of St. Mary's, Primrose Hill, he pointed during the sermon to a run of crotchets and quavers in some florid eighteenth century tune and said: "My 'eart leaps up when I be'old ay rainbow in thee sky!" He was an Inspector of Schools and deplored the singing by assembled children of pietistic hymns to German-style tunes. "Leave, ah leave me not alone"—that from youngsters on a Sunday summer morning, said Geoffrey Shaw, indicated a complete indifference to religion, common sense, or young minds. He thought Dykes's tune rather better than most because, although not suitable for school assembly, it had some sense of melody and feeling. He specified the tunes he most disliked for what he called their "minimity"—"As if the hierarchy had ordained that each pew should be filled by four round and pasty-faced old men, none replaced by a couple of merry little brunettes". His pet aversions were *Mannheim* ("Lead us heavenly Father") and *Culbach*. His reason for prejudice against the latter makes a story worth telling in his own words to enliven this rather dull chapter.

You know I quite liked being taken to church in those days when we had no radio or gramophone. I so loved the singing and the organ when I was six that they went on taking me, and as soon as I could read I used to spend the prayers and sermon times looking up what hymns were "coming" from the numbers on the board. One day I could hardly wait for No. 547—"Children of the Heavenly King as ye journey sweetly sing". This must surely be a marvellous tune, for the words conjured up the picture of our summer "walking day" when we had a grand outdoor procession with a band and the mayor and the bigwigs, and men on horses and the girls carrying flowers, and we boys in our best clothes ... and I imagined us waving to our admiring parents at the doors and windows and the farm gates as we passed. So I managed to contain myself even through the Litany without misbehaviour. At last No. 547 was announced and the organ played over the tune. All my hopes were dashed and my dreams ruined. What do you think was considered the fit expression for that heavenly pageant? *Culbach* my lad! Out came the static minims ... VON, two, sree, four ... you must admit that for sheer desperation of invention the second line takes the biscuit.

It is true that the Germanophile Victorians were very much influenced by Lutheran books, for most Victorian musicians were Leipzig trained, or studied under teachers who had studied in Germany. By Bach's day genuinely Lutheran

Culbach

Ex. 22

chorales had already been "ironed out" into staid "minimity". These were translations of the ordinary of the Mass and of the Canticles—called the "Catechism chorales" because they were in such frequent use that children were taught them by heart—together with the *Detemporelieder* or office hymns for the main Sundays and Holy Days in the year. Yet like the older Calvinistic psalmody, these ancient chorales retained something of their vigour even in the eighteenth century form, though we must allow for prejudice towards them that comes from our imagining them with Bachian harmony; but most Lutheran church music from Bach to the end of the nineteenth century was decorously dull.[1] It was normally so even in Hamburg, Berlin or Leipzig at churches associated with fine music on special occasions, or with scholars who secured revivals of works by Palestrina, Schütz or Bach. The standard of its pedestrian hymnody may be guessed when we remember that the editors of our standard English collections have combed most of the German books in use up to 1900 and taken from them the more attractive tunes—for instance :

Lübeck from Freylinghausen's *Gesangbuch* of 1704 (*A. and M.* 38)

Swabia from Spiess's *Gesangbuch* of 1745

Franconia from König's *Gesangbuch* of 1738 (*A. and M.* 335)

Ratisbon from Werne's *Choralbuch* of 1815 (*A. and M.* 7)

Ellacombe from a Mainz book of 1833 (*A. and M.* 132).

The exceptions to dullness are few. *Mendelssohn* ("Hark the herald angels sing") actually roused objections from the composer whose name it bears; it was an adaptation by W. H. Cummings of a chorus in Mendelssohn's *Festgesang*, first included in a hymn book by Chope in 1856. Another exception is *Barton* by J. H. Knecht in a Stuttgart book of 1799 (*A. and M.* 289).

It is possible that Scandinavian and Finnish Lutheran hymn books have not yet been sifted by British or American collectors. I know a fine tune by Leevi Madetoja (1887–1947), a prolific composer in all genres, regarded in Finland as second only to Sibelius. The tune I know is set to a Finnish version of Walsham How's "For all the saints" in the same metre as the original. It is immensely popular in Finland and, since it admirably suits the English words, would be so here

[1] For general commentary on the German Evangelical Church see Chapter 1.

if the hymn were already not known by at least two fine settings (though I regard Madetoja's as finer than either).

WELSH HYMNS

The nineteenth century saw the most prolific flowering of Welsh hymnody, though the flowers never seem quite as fine when they are transplanted as they do in their native soil. (Which may explain why Madetoja's "For all the saints" and other Scandinavian tunes have not travelled.) They scarcely travelled at all even among Calvinists and Methodists before Welshmen came to hold positions in England which gave them an influence on church music, whatever their private beliefs and disbeliefs. The first was Hubert Parry, Principal of the R.C.M. and Professor at Oxford, the next R. Vaughan Williams, music editor of *E. H.*, and the third H. Walford Davies, powerful in several appointments, such as that of organist of the Temple Church, but supremely powerful as the most successful pedagogic musician of the B.B.C. before the days of television.

Vaughan Williams put some twenty Welsh tunes in the first *E. H.* (1906), and to this day only *Aberystwyth, Cwm Rhondda* (much loved by the armed forces during two wars) *St. Denio, Ebenezer, Hyfrydol, Llanfair* and *Gwalchmai* are widely known across the Severn. Every one of these was composed in the nineteenth century and most of them when already Welsh organists and choirmasters were influenced by English (i.e. German) classical harmony and melody.

There are at least one or two even finer Welsh tunes than those already familiar outside Wales; one is quoted at Ex. 23 to prove the point, for though it has a place in all the current non-anglican books in Britain it is by no means widely familiar outside Wales.

The best of these Welsh tunes make most English Methodist and anglican nineteenth century tunes seem to have no more colour than the church-shop Trinity antependium that was once green and gold but has faded to dusty olive and dull brown-yellow: yet they were first composed in the 1760s when Methodism made its tremendous impact upon a Wales which suffered greatly from the abuses (such as absentee bishops) of the corrupt established church. The largest number of these nationally distinctive tunes is therefore used by the "Calvinistic Methodists"—a designation which might seem paradoxical to the theological student but for his recollection of Whitefield's brand of Methodism. The high-churchmanship of the Wesleys themselves seems to have had little effect on Wales until the present century, during which it has become

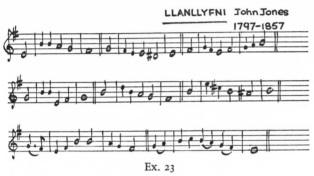

Ex. 23

the prevailing "colour" of the Church of Wales—the episcopal church, separated from the Church of England only by the disestablishment fulfilled in 1912. By that year it had accepted English cathedral music for a preponderantly English ritual, together with *A. and M.* and *E. H.* (the latter being a much favoured hymn book in Wales) with some of their content available in Welsh as well as English. This means that only a small fraction of distinctive Welsh hymnody (most of it consisting of tunes known in England because they were set to English words) has crossed from Calvinistic Methodist chapels to "church" congregations, even for services held in Welsh.

Certain features of Welsh tunes which make them refreshingly welcome to ears satiated with chorales and English hymns also make them recalcitrant to English translations; these features include the frequently anapaestic or trochaic scansion, irregular metres, and the arching of the melody to climax by sequences (or semi-sequences) set to repetitions of a short line, often the penultimate line. Surely, however, the effect of Welsh tunes is as much attributable to their singers as to their music.

Until Anglicans and Episcopalians generally (except artisan or rustic Roman Catholics, such as those in Ireland or Bavaria) change their attitude to congregational music it is not to be deplored that the characteristic Welsh tunes continue in "chapel" and do not get into "church". For all the talk about hearty participation, episcopal congregations make precious little effort to sing. They may be whipped up to slight effort for a special occasion, such as broadcast hymn-singing, but in the average parish church they fall back into their musical apathy within a week of the special rousing. Methodist churches in England have become just as timid or snobbish-sophisticated as Anglican, and we must go to a Welsh "Little Bethel" to hear fulfilled Wesley's injunctions "Sing *every word*. Sing *the meaning* of each word. Take breath before each sentence etc." In the Welsh chapel, as in the country and small-town churches of catholic Rhineland, a fine sound of fearless voices drowns a small organ, and I would rather hear that effect than the sound of a magnificent organ and salaried organist making two-thirds or more of what is miscalled congregational music in the suburban churches of London, Berlin or Stuttgart.

Note. A few comments upon the hymnody of the larger nonconformist churches of this country and upon that of the Roman Church are more conveniently made at the end of the next chapter than here.

7

Congregational Music

Since naturally it is British music that most often receives attention from music historians writing in English I have tried not to give it disproportionate space here. I was not tempted to do so when dealing with nineteenth century choir music which for us now is of hardly more than documentary importance; more interesting than its quality is its enormous quantity, the demand for which that quantity was supplied and the religious movements, including a religious romantic revival which affected the simple as well as the cultured and multiplied church choirs in cities and hamlets. When we reach congregational music I am tempted to swell a chapter into a book, however well others writers have dealt with the subject, and it is not chauvinism that fills the pen and concentrates attention upon Great Britain, but the fact that, since the chorales provided by Luther and his musical friends for the German Churches and people there has been no finer treasury of popular hymnody than the Victorians garnered into the first issue of *Hymns Ancient and Modern* in 1861 and into its subsequent supplements. I am not thinking only of the metrical psalms, Methodist and other tunes from former collections which the editors brought into that book but of hymns contributed *ad hoc* by themselves and others; some were to new verses and some to verses like many in Keble's *The Christian Year* which had been previously used for devotional reading, not congregational singing.

In most parts of the midlands and north, as well as in Wales, hymns supplemented or ousted metrical psalms before the middle of the century. They received a kind of official acceptance, though it is difficult to know on what grounds they needed it, when in 1821 the Archbishop of York paid from his private purse for the reprinting of a revised edition of the collection made by Thomas Cotterill, a Sheffield clergyman whose congregation had objected to the foisting of his book upon them. Before the New Version of metrical psalms was finally superseded in the established church by *A. and M.* it was normally printed with a few hymns for times and seasons—Morning, Evening, Christmas, Easter, Holy Communion, etc. We may easily forget that Bishop Heber's *Hymns written and adapted to the Weekly Service of the Year*, published by his widow, and Keble's *The Christian Year* both appeared in 1827, six years before Keble's assize sermon and thirty-four years before *A. and M.* Only a fraction of either publication found tunes in standard hymnaries, but each author's literary standard and anglican bias (the insistence upon the liturgical Kalendar and sacramental doctrine) are manifest.

THE SECRET OF VICTORIAN HYMNODY

Perhaps that is why most of the Tractarians turned champions of hymnody, but they were also attracted to it because of their interest in the worship of the primitive, the Byzantine and the medieval church. For them the nation-wide acceptance of *A. and M.* was a triumph. The years surrounding 1861 saw the issue of Neale's splendid translations from the Latin and of translations by others from the German; Frances Cox's *Sacred Hymns from the German* appeared in 1841 and Catherine Winkworth's *Chorale Book for England* in 1863. The apt title *Ancient and Modern* could not have been justly claimed by any previous collection any more than *Far and Wide* unless the implied stretch of time were a couple of centuries and of space a couple of lands; the 1861 title could stand even when more of the nineteenth than any other century came into the much enlarged *A. and M.* on which most Anglicans were nurtured during the early years of the twentieth century.

Neale's standing as a scholar and poet has only recently received adequate recognition, and then naturally by a few connoisseurs. Hymnal compilers have far from done justice to his original verses as distinct from his free translations. As far as I know, for instance, "There is a stream", which could adorn the book of almost any denomination from Roman to Unitarian, has been used only in *Songs of Syon* (1910), perhaps because only Woodward and Palmer, belonging to a religious community, were scholars of Neale's calibre. I quote here two verses of this particular hymn to support my claims for it. There is no need for good hymns even to approach fine poetry, but some of Neale's are none the less serviceable as hymns for being genuine poems. His translation "O Unity of three-fold light" (*E. H.* 163) so perfectly fits Tallis's famous Third Mode Melody as to make the alliance of that melody with Addison's subjective "When rising from the bed of death" (*E. H.* 92) seem forced. Addison's language belongs too much to his own time to go well with music which the least knowledgeable must feel to be much more ancient than modern. As for Neale's "There is a stream", it so perfectly fits the six-line and superior version of Gibbons's "Song 9" (to which it is set in *Songs of Syon*) as to make one wish that there had been no four-line version despite its splendid alliance with "Forth in thy name O Lord I go".

> There is a stream whose waters rise
> Amidst the hills of Paradise,
> Where foot of man hath never trod,
> Proceeding from the throne of God,
> O give me sickness here, or strife,
> So I may reach that spring of life.

> There is a rock that nigh at hand
> Gives shadow in a weary land;
> Who in that stricken rock hath rest
> Finds waters gushing from its breast.
> O grant me when this scene is o'er
> Their lot who thirst not any more.

I would not extol words in a book about music if it were not that the words, which get better as hymn material as the verses proceed, are of exactly the kind for music, and show how deeply the religious movements of the nineteenth century united rare and fastidious souls like Neale, at least in artistic sentiments, with more ordinary people. It has been said that there is a cosy respectability about Victorian hymnody, the tunes of such people as Dykes and Monk and the words they favoured being parallel with such albums as those of Mendelssohn's *Songs without Words* and the pretty or morally improving lithographs and colour prints which went on the walls of small houses as well as great. I do not propose to contest this opinion for it is a subjective one which I happen to share when I read it; I am too much the child of Victorian lower middle class ancestors to be aware of this reaction until it is suggested; but I still want to know why it is a fault of Victorian hymnody to reflect the feelings of the new democracy, why the beautifully fashioned, useful and cleverly picturesque *Songs without Words* should be matter for less gratitude than attempts at Beethoven rhetoric or Berlioz melodic adventure. I also remember Vaughan Williams's chapter heading "Bach, the Great Bourgeois" and the annoyance it first gave me as an over-simplified half-truth. In the same book of essays comes the phrase "Music's a rum go"; it is the art that least engages the intellect yet most reveals, both in composer and listener, the total man. It is therefore the most dangerous one from which to make logical or sociological deductions. The most aristocratic of musicians (I mean when composing to please himself) was Mozart, who makes temporarily an aristocrat of everyone who delights in his highly stylised expression; yet Mozart, like his father, was decidedly bourgeois, class conscious and sensitive to the distinction between independent citizen and gentleman's gentleman or employer's utter dependant.

Of course Victorian hymnody reflects desire for cosiness and respectability more than most hymnody because it was produced when the desire and the chance of fulfilling it affected millions during the growth of democracy. It ill becomes us to despise the Victorians on this account. Is our religion less cosy and respectable than theirs, less middle-classy and cultured-classy in anything but pulpit and church-organisation talk about "relevance", cant phrases about "the office, the workshop and the factory" and sentimental symbolism like the bringing of tools or embroideries representing industries into church—the respectable, staid, cosy church that feels all the more cosy by contemplation of grimmer things outside? We *talk*, even sing, about being up and doing, and there would be no harm in that healthy self-accusation and self-rousing for Monday and Tuesday if we were not hypocritical enough to think ourselves superior to the Victorians who openly regarded public worship as a refuge and sang "O paradise, O paradise!" In the longed-for Paradise, Jerusalem, Galilee—whatever the symbol was—there was cosiness in the home and arms of God, and respectability which gave security from poverty and oppression. Except in the arts, the creation of men's imagination, the expression of their aspirations, the Victorian age was one of rigours for most people who included in their worship the contemplation of Heaven's cosiness and respectability. It was by no means the whole of their religion. Most church folk fasted, prayed, read and gave alms better than we do. Most forms of employment on Monday were wearisome and health-sapping, hours were long, winter was still to be feared, wealth and rank could inflict misery on those without them, men and women could obey their employers or starve, and starvation was not uncommon; age had no pension, sickness was costly, disability tragic, surgery terrible, domestic duties a drudgery, child mortality and death in childbirth frequent. Dickens is not merely a caricaturist nor his beadles, schoolmasters, lawyers, petty employers, arrogant squires and nasty parvenus merely the creatures of his fancy. To arraign the Victorians for expressing yearnings after cosiness and respectability is as unintelligent as to arraign medieval poets for being ecstatic about the arrival of spring.

A NEW JUDGMENT

As far as I know I hold highly in regard the bulk of Victorian hymns not merely out of sentimental recollections and associations, but after trying to judge them as should a professional musician bound by his appointments to note their effectiveness in churches and schools. It is perhaps fortunate that I am unable to judge music that I know too well; it ceases to mean to me anything comparable with artistic experience. I cannot tell whether Monk's "Abide with me" is good or not: I did not recognise the excellence of Dykes's *Nicea* to "Holy, Holy, Holy" until late in life, for it was too often sung when I was young and when I was allowed to choose hymns I resolutely omitted it from church lists. Twenty years ago I came to Dykes's own church where it was sung once a year, on Trinity Sunday and followed by *Te Deum*, also heard by most worshippers at St. Oswald's only on that festival. (I am not advocating this extension of the normal material to be regarded as *proprium de tempore* but witnessing to one effect of the practice.) Nor am I anxious here to praise what are already generally recognised as fine tunes; rather do I ask for a fresh examination of many which have either fallen into neglect or become despised after over-use.

Let me begin with a hymn of which many must have wearied at school, in church, certainly in the armed forces— Wesley's "Soldiers of Christ arise !" as set in the 1861 *A. and M.* to Monk's *St. Ethelwald*. It is usually sung much too fast. Let it be sung slowly and grandly as if it were a Bach chorale—go now to the piano and play it so. How well it suits the words! Are you counting a whole three beats for Monk's pause at the end of the third line which was restored in *E. H.*? Are its vocal lines inferior to those of most Bach chorales? (This is not a question to apply to every hymn tune; Bach wrote his best parts to the dullest tunes, which we often suppose to be less than dull because we recall them with his harmonies.) Let us turn to a good tune in which the middle parts have little "horizontal" interest but are simply the efficient choral fillings of the chord progressions. Elvey's *Diademata*, composed for Matthew Bridges's "Crown him with many crowns" when it went into the 1861 book, is exactly the sort of Victorian tune to be called vulgar or pedestrian by the gourmets of church music if they are so unintelligent as to judge hymns as pabulum for their fastidious palates. I did not regard as unintelligent the cathedral organist who recently told me that he was not at all interested in hymns, and added "What *is* a good hymn?" Before returning to Elvey's *Diademata* let us attempt to answer his question —that particular question, not "What is a great or wonderful hymn like *Lasst uns erfreuen, Pange lingua, Vexilla regis*, or Gibbons's *Song 1, Song 22* or *Song 24*?"

A good hymn is one that wears well, makes the simple folk enjoy its words and remember those words because of the musical appeal, yet is not found contemptible by the musically educated and half-educated. It is congregational yet not wearisome for choirs. Like all worthy music it *seems* to have been composed spontaneously. These conditions are surely fulfilled by *Diademata* and by Elvey's other good tune, *St. George's Windsor* which the *A. and M.* editors for some strange reason took away from its excellent words, "Hark, the song of jubilee" and put to the harvest hymn "Come ye thankful people, come". Both these tunes are classics, for classics are not given their status by commissions or councils; they become classics because people take them to their hearts while they neglect other works of their kind. I have seen each of these two Elvey tunes put to three different sets of verses. I last saw *Diademata* on a card, sent with 1,000 copies for distribution among students with the request that they would sing it at "United Nations Meetings". I threw them away because the verses were so vile and Elvey's notes had to be halved to accommodate them, as in the first line, "WE are un-NI-ted NAY-shuns". Plainly Elvey's hymn tunes have a gusto and memorability which his cathedral pieces lack, and the same remark could be passed about the compositions of others who entered the musical pantheon in 1861. Naïvety, vulgarity and sentimentality are not essential to popular music. They may be found in verse or tune and still leave the total hymn finer than a chaste one which sounds less spontaneous.

The good hymn cannot be produced without faith in hymns whatever faith its author and composer have in traditional doctrines. Without faith the most accomplished composer may fail to secure the hit that was achieved time after time by Monk and Dykes. Even when his muse is lyrical the fine poet may not be able to produce good verses for hymns. Matthew Bridges's "Crown him with many crowns" comes near to poetry in most verses, but we must accept the bathos of its last line and no more presume to clean up the Victorians than we should clean up the words or music of Schubert's songs. Ambitious poetry and music can be positively dangerous in hymns and it is when Bridges has waxed too sublime that he prepares the last line flop.

> Glassed in a sea of light
> Whose everlasting waves
> Reflect his throne—the Infinite!
> Who lives and loves and saves.

Surely musicians who misjudge Victorian hymns make the mistake of divorcing tunes from words. That is why too many of them think they have done us a service by putting words that were allied with a contemporary or near-contemporary Victorian tune to some refined piece by Schütz,

Gibbons or Bach. Despite the many tunes that are acceptable to more than one hymn, a tune is the better for seeming to have been called forth to serve one set of words. The conditions were well fulfilled in the 1868 reprint of *A. and M.* by the alliance of *Horsley* with Mrs. Alexander's "There is a green hill". The verses date from a children's book of 1848 and the tune from a collection of twenty-four psalms issued by W. Horsley in 1844. Here again is a fine hymn that has been cheapened by speed of singing and general over-use, and I ask it to be given the treatment I advocated for *St. Ethelwald.* Let it be sung slowly and solemnly and restricted to Passiontide. People might attend a course of lectures on the Redemption and engage in much devotional reading upon the subject and still come no nearer to faith in the means of our salvation than by the slow and firm singing of Mrs. Alexander's simple, very plain and simple words. The verses are of no great literary merit because they state doctrine simply, and the stuff of doctrine is not the stuff of high poetry. Metaphorically, however, it may be said that the experience of great poetry comes from the devout singing of these words with their music. Plain verses and pedestrian music glow as the dull filament at the charge of power. Only a fool pretends that Victorian hymnody, or for that matter the great Lutheran hymnody, is like that so-called folk song in which we may meet fine poetry and fine melody in its own right, composed by the finest artists, not in court and monastery, but among those who were not trained to write down their conceptions. Victorian hymnody is not folk music but semi-sophisticated popular music in which we may meet phrases and bits of tune or harmony unconsciously borrowed from famous poets and musicians. (If there were space I could prove that Dr. Dykes knew *Don Giovanni* very well though the fact is not mentioned in his surviving letters.) Victorian hymnody is still valid for us, that is to say that we can use it without such falsehood as our singing of negro spirituals in imitation of their dialect and as though we were members of an oppressed race. We do not know for how long it will remain valid—when it will be sung or played for the pleasure of period-fancying; but it is the testimony of thousands, not only in Britain and America, that they would be deprived of much expression of the otherwise inexpressible if they were denied Victorian hymns.

SINCERE OR SENTIMENTAL?

We find the artistic vitality and genuineness of Victorian hymns upheld in no less august a compilation than *The Oxford History of Music*. In charge of the last, the seventh volume of that European survey of all music, was Dr. H. C. Colles, a gracious and an unusually perceptive man who would not have denied that, writing in the 1930s, and being a friend both of Robert Bridges, editor of *The Yattendon Hymnal* and also of Vaughan Williams of *The English Hymnal*, he shared their natural reaction against much in the Victorian ethos. It is therefore remarkable that Colles had very little to say about church music in general in his short chapter "England 1850–1900" yet devoted two pages to "the hymns of the people" which "cannot be passed over in a country where the Church was the only established institution charged officially with the duty of making music". He uses most of these two pages in defence of Dykes who, though he "composed too much and too readily" after his first successes of 1861, has since been wrongly dismissed as though most of his work were sentimental and inferior. "The injustice of the estimate is at once apparent when it is recalled that his modest contribution of seven tunes to the book of 273 hymns published in 1861 included six which have become inseparable from favourite hymns. Only one, written to the *Dies Irae* . . . cannot be said to have become a classic."

J. B. DYKES

"Sentimental" should denote the falsehood of imitated or affected sentiment, yet it has been often applied where neither the popular touch, the homeliness, nor the strong emotion is affected and false, but existed from the first in the thoughts of the author and composer. I have myself made this mistake and been led by a better mind than mine to reverse my opinion. As a boy I grew weary of "Nearer my God to thee" at evening services, for it is not the sort of hymn to appeal to the young. One day in 1960 I happened to say to Sir Jack Westrup that the progression shown at Ex. 25 in Dykes's *Horbury* was remarkable for its period. I should not have been surprised at the Oxford Professor's comment but at the time I was. He said: "That is one of the best hymns ever written. Sarah Adams's verses make an almost perfect lyric and Dykes's tune is their admirable counterpart." To talk of "sugary chromatics" and "cheap vulgarity" as if they were the chief characteristics of Monk, Dykes, Elvey, Gauntlett, Smart, Havergal, Redhead and the other hard survivors from the first issues of *Hymns Ancient and Modern* is to repeat shallow judgments without verifying facts. It would be equally shallow to deny the frequent occurrence of these faults in some of the best Victorian hymnodists, for they are also found in very great composers. I said I would not defend Victorian hymns by pointing to the great ones, like Dykes's *Nicea*. I wonder how many of readers even *know* his *Lux vera*. I quote the tune along with its opening words at Ex. 24. It appeared in the Second Supplement of *A. and M.* and I marvel that it was not included in the revised edition of 1950 or, for that matter, in books of all denominations from Unitarian to Roman Catholic. Perhaps it reveals so little of unfashionable Victorian traits that it also reveals nothing for the period connoisseur. Verses and tune are beautifully unpretentious, a very different matter from lacking character.[1]

I have fixed upon Dykes not simply because I live where the fruits of his goodness as a minister to working folk can still be seen but because, being along with Monk the most popular of Victorian church tunesmiths, he has received the

[1] The hymn will be found at No. 687 in *Ancient and Modern* (Standard Edition).

heaviest lashing from twentieth century reaction. No wonder that Dr. Routley in *The Music of Christian Hymnody*[1] fixes upon him to represent the virtues and defects of "Victorian Composers" in his chapter of that heading. Dykes was usually most feeble when he forced himself to oblige his friends of

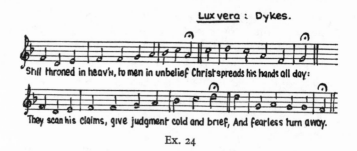

Lux vera : Dykes.

Still throned in heav'n, to men in unbelief Christ spreads his hands all day:
They scan his claims, give judgment cold and brief, And fearless turn away.

Ex. 24

Horbury: Dykes

Ex. 25

all denominations and compose tunes which did not "come" at the bidding of words. His failures as well as his successes show him to have been a priest first and a composer a long way afterwards. How well this is shown in his setting of Newman's "Praise to the Holiest" which hovers between poetry and priestly instruction, each first line to a verse being an apostrophe in the style of Charles Wesley. Dykes's *Gerontius* exactly parallels Newman's verses. There is no bathos, but the power of the first line sets a strain that cannot be held. Even so I am tired of people who object to every one of

[1] Independent Press, London, 1957.

Dykes's and other men's pedal basses, as if only one ideal of vocal harmony—that of the seventeenth century or of Bach —could serve a good hymn. The four strokes on the same bass note at the opening of *Gerontius* form a springboard for the memorable second and third bars. A similar effect is secured in *St. Oswald* and I see no reason why an effect admired in a Beethoven overture should be despised when it gives the association of drum strokes in a militant hymn like "Through the night of doubt and sorrow". Not that the procedure was always commendable. It makes no springboard at the opening of Dykes's vulgar old screamer *Alford* to "Ten thousand times ten thousand" which can be sung a whole *fourth* lower and then touch only middle B for its lowermost note! (It would then lose almost the only point it has, the colouring of the words by high notes.)

The sooner *Gerontius* is restored to "Praise to the Holiest" the better. As music *Richmond* (the normal alternative in Britain) is one of our outstandingly fine tunes but in some churches it has been debased, along with *Melcombe* and *Wareham*, into a stand-by. Shaw's *Marching* is not a bad tune for "Through the night of doubt and sorrow" and its composer had the good sense to use nineteenth century harmonies for nineteenth century verses; but *Marching* wears no better than most of Shaw's tunes and Shaw would have done better to make a good tune to verses that lack one. *Marching* is not a better tune than *St. Oswald* for those words. The gusto, the reminiscence of a miners' brass band, no doubt the very element which the *English Hymnal* editors disliked in Dykes's tune is just what should commend it. That is not one of Dykes's "stagnant" basses, and I have never heard a congregation sounding in the least stagnant when allowed this tune. It goes with a zip. As one of the *E. H.* directors I am unlikely to be other than enthusiastic for the new standards set up by that book in 1906, and I should like readers to know that Vaughan Williams himself lived long enough to believe that, though it was right in 1906 to oust so many Victorian tunes, the contents of the "chamber of horrors" (the appendix into which alternative tunes were put if it was thought that some churches would not accept certain new ones) was due for re-examination. He once said: "I so love Dykes the man that I wish I liked more of his tunes, but I like only three." Before he died he had "come round" to *Gerontius* and *Dominus regit me*, having previously liked only *Nicea*, *St. Cross* and, curiously enough, *Lux benigna*. The idea of the "chamber of horrors" was to make it inconvenient to use "the other tune" which "will be found in the Appendix". Vaughan Williams was modest enough and honest enough to defer to my wish (in editing the music of the *English Hymnal Service Book*, 1962) that either "the other tune" should not be printed at all, or it should be provided with its words so that choirs were not forced to flick the pages back and forth between words and appendix tune. He also opposed the common criticism that too many Victorian tunes were like part-songs and written for choirs. Provided that congregations took to the melody and could manage it the more a non-unison tune interested parish choirs the better.

Following those original *E. H.* editors have we not too often judged hymn tunes purely as melodies? The *E. H.* choice has led many to associate "The King of love" with *St. Columba*, a beautiful Irish melody first introduced to England by Stanford. With a piano and children's voices and as a unison tune it is as superior to Dykes's *Dominus regit me* as some of the original melodies which Bach called *Arien* in Schemelli's book are superior to some of the staid chorales he inherited. The most notable exceptions among the chorales, such as *Innsbruck*, were often derived from secular songs. If tunes like *St. Columba* should be harmonised at all, their lilt makes them inferior to Victorian tunes for big gatherings of choir and congregation, and hopeless for open air singing with bands. The proof is in the sound. I have never heard a large gathering raise the full throated unison to *St. Columba* that it does to *Dominus regit me*.

'HYMNS ANCIENT AND MODERN'

Scarcely a single hymn or tune in low church rivals to *Hymns Ancient and Modern* survives on artistic grounds. I say this without prejudice of churchmanship for possibly the nadir of bad church music is found in *The Mirfield Mission Hymn Book*—a fact which has to be remembered by those who rightly claim for another anglo-catholic book, *Songs of Syon*, that it is musically superior to any English collection. (*Songs of Syon* appeals so exclusively to the educated and cultured worshipper that it is utterly impracticable for most parish churches, grateful though every church musician should be for its presence on his shelves.) Few hymns from any nineteenth century nonconformist collection published after *A. and M.* are of considerable merit; the best ones in *The Methodist Hymn Book* (1933) came there under the musical editorship of Dr. Luke Wiseman, a notable President of the Conference. Nearly all the worthy contents of these books are also found in *A. and M.* but it must be remembered that much of the finest nonconformist hymnody went into *A. and M.*, and still more was to go later into *E. H.* On what grounds have we any right to deprecate the sentimental or vulgar hymns in these collections while saying nothing to attack Revivalist hymnody, either in the forms generally called "Old Methodist" or in their late nineteenth century equivalents, the "Sacred Songs and Solos" of Moody and Sankey? The test is the eternal one of sincerity or falsehood. However sincere be the wish to save souls the artistic means is not justified by the worthiness of the end if the user of the means deliberately uses upon others what is not naturally his own expression. It is less false for the educated parson to use in his sermons the archaic "Dearly beloved" than to talk of "You chaps" and thereby be guilty of the bad manners of patronising his hearers, showing his self-conscious awareness of a difference of intelligence and status between them and him. He commits the same offence if he provides for them music which he himself does not love. The saloon and music-hall idioms of melody, rhythm and shape generally, and the limited harmonies that could be learnt upon an accordion within two lessons—these represent the taste of the missioners themselves as well as that of their unchurched audiences. The naïvety is all of a piece with the crude preaching and extempore praying of Moody and Sankey; when this art is taken over by the Oxford and Cambridge evangelists and retreat holders of the Anglican Church and forced upon their trained organists, choirs and congregations *via* the *Mirfield Mission Hymn Book* or that damnable part of *E. H.* called "Missions" by deliberate condescension there is found only pseudo-naïvety as disgusting as the pretended lisping of a courtesan . . . unless, of course, we can make it the object of humour, as we do mademoiselle's allurements. It is probable that derision will oust falsity, in these old guises or in the guise of "beat groups", spirituals and imitations of linguistic or musical dialects, far more quickly than angry protesting.

ROMAN CATHOLIC HYMNS

Except in those parts of Germany where for centuries Roman Catholics had seen to it that their protestant compatriots did not enjoy their hymnody exclusively the Roman Church does not seem to have added many great hymns to the general treasury during the nineteenth century. Yet one must retain the safe "seem" because in England there was no collection corresponding with the large volumes used by other denominations; as in Latin countries still, there were only small collections licensed for diocesan use and often bound with missals or other books of devotion such as "The Garden of the Soul". The first very widely used hymn book of Roman Catholics in England (I do not know about Ireland) was not issued until 1901—*Arundel Hymns*, edited by the Duke of Norfolk and Charles Gatty. In it are one or two good hymns which not only found their way into *The Westminster Hymnal*, edited by Terry in 1912 and conservatively revised in 1940, but also into *E. H.* and many other twentieth century books. Supposing that first the Duke of Norfolk and then Terry took the best hymns from diocesan and local books they must have been richer than protestant collections in good Christmas tunes, both British and continental, and also in French diocesan melodies of the seventeenth and early eighteenth centuries set to Horatian metres and originally to both Latin and vernacular words. The chief disappointment in catholic books of this period comes from the section dealing with the Blessed Sacrament in which we should expect much worth exchanging; but evidently the editors of *A. and M.* had already helped themselves here, especially to the best hymns of ancient origin, and it must be remembered that protestant— indeed even unitarian—tunes were used in nineteenth century Roman Catholic books although words by Protestants were forbidden there.

This discrimination between the sources of verses and tunes is clearly stated in the preface to *Arundel Hymns*. Its effect upon converts must often have been mildly surprising. For instance they can surely never have heard *Nun danket* to any other words than some translation of the words originally inspiring Crüger's chorale, e.g. "Now thank we all our God", but they might hear it in Roman churches to sacramental and Marian hymns. The *E. H.* editors were not the first to put *Richmond* to Newman's "Praise to the Holiest" with which it is associated in *Arundel Hymns* and called "Old English Melody". (Deliberately? Were its unitarian associations known to His Grace?) In *The Westminster Hymnal* Newman's verses found a splendid tune by Terry himself, but Terry evidently dared not oust some of the cruder and more sentimental sacramental and Marian hymns which now meet clerical disapproval in many quarters and are generally referred to, not quite justly, as "Irish hymns". One may sympathise with Terry for it must have been known that his main sources for good tunes and words would perforce have been Protestant and he was working in days far less tolerant than these when protestant editors would have feared to include even tunes which were known to be favourites in Roman churches. His chief difficulty was that there was no great hymn tradition comparable to the German and the English in Italy where *inno* denotes a composition rather like our Sunday School "anthem" with a little instrumental introduction and a somewhat florid tune in the style of a

A. Inno eucaristico : F. Taveni.

In- ni e can-ti seo-glia-mo fe-de-li, al Di-

vi-no eu-ca-ri-sti-co Rè. E-glia-sco-so nei mistici ve-li

B. Canzonscina pasquale

Cri-sto ri-su-sci- ti in tut-ti i cuo- ri !

Ex. 26

national anthem—Mussolini's jolly *Giovinezza*, enjoyed by our troops during the war as much as the ridiculous Horst Wessel Song, was called *Inno trionfale*.

One hears *inni* chiefly at processions, either round churches or more often outside them, but they are much used during services too. What we call a hymn is known as a *canzonscina* unless its style is very German and it is then called *corale*. In the Verona diocese I often heard "O salutaris hostia" sung to Hanover (the second and third notes made into one for 'sal-') and when I went to the organ to look at the music I found it called *corale*, given no name, but bearing the proud legend 'Haendel'! I am bound to say that most *canzonscine* I have heard, even in cathedrals and seminaries, are of a kind all too common in our own books of various denominations, the kind which the English hierarchy would class with "Irish hymns"; the exceptions are chiefly of Calvinistic or Lutheran origin. The more popular *inni* do not offend one any more than does the Moody and Sankey idiom among poor folk in a missioners' marquee or a tin tabernacle. In a country whose poorest folk love romantic opera as football is loved here the jaunty martial rhythms or tender ariette melodies of *inni* do not sound false. I give two specimens at Ex. 26, one of an *inno* and one of a *canzonscina pasquale* taken from the most popular book used in the Naples area. The *canzonscina* will surely be recognised by most readers, and it is greatly to our shame that it would not be recognised by all our church-folk even if played and sung to them. Before we think our-selves superior to Naples at least let us concede that Naples knows the greatest of all Easter hymns and most of us do not.

"YOU ALL DID LOVE HIM ONCE"

The close of our survey brings us to our starting point. The most considerable achievement of the nineteenth century was its advance to what is called democracy; whether in fact this is politically a misnomer or not, there is in democratic coun-tries greater freedom than at any time before 1800 to move, accept or reject opinion on matters from religion and govern-ment to food and clothing and, in Newman's words, "to choose and see one's path". It is natural, therefore, that the most remarkable characteristic of the arts in the nineteenth century should be their democratisation. Posterity may find the contribution of the nineteenth century to theatre music (not only in "grand" opera) and to domestic music more important than its fine symphonies and concertos; undoubtedly its most important contribution to church music was in popular hymnody. And since this was the century of the romantic revival in the arts, both that hymnody and the more ambitious choir and organ music went with the roman-

F

ticising of public worship, even in supposedly austere denominations. Against much of that romanticising we are now
supposedly in reaction, and it is fortunate that, in declining
to use music we dislike, we do not destroy irrevocably as we
do if we want buildings or decorations to be superseded. How
many treasures of the past have been destroyed not by savages,
nor during war, but by men of taste who thought them
barbarous and out of fashion?

It must have been noticed, surely, that in these pages I
have sedulously avoided the phrases "bad taste" and "good
taste". There are no doubt circumstances and contexts in
which they can be aptly and profitably used but to the historian
they are often matter for amusement. Had we been contemporaries of Burney, that is to say of J. S. Bach's sons, our
"good taste" would have been to avoid performing or using
most of the music of Bach, Handel and Rameau. Their taste
was matter for ridicule long before they were dead. Today
"good taste" too frequently means "our taste" or "my taste"
which, even if it is sincere, even if the liking and disliking
it savours seems uninfluenced by deference to the tastes of
the wealthy, or the mighty in their seats behind their micro-
phones and in the offices of newspapers and periodicals, is
rarely as purely personal as we think it. We admire other
men unless we are very mean or very unfortunate and their
judgments cannot but affect our taste. The men whom I most
admired when I was a young man were sincerely harsh in
many of their opinions about music and other arts of the
nineteenth century, and their reasons for their opinions seemed
convincing even when I felt to some hero of my boyhood,
like César Franck, as did Anthony to the other Caesar—"You
all did love him once". The illusions of first love towards the
nineteenth century are past for most of us, and it has receded
far enough into history for us no longer to treat our reactions
to its art as a mere matter of the good or bad taste of today
—the most tasteless age there had ever been. We can now
examine its music just as music. Some of it is magnificent.

Index